Good
Old-Fashioned
Cookies

Also by Susan Kosoff

Good Old-Fashioned Cakes
Cooking with Five Ingredients or Less (co-written with Teresa Kennedy)

Good Old-Fashioned Cookies

More than Eighty Classic Cookie Recipes– Updated for Today's Bakers

Susan Kosoff

Illustrations by Diana Thewlis

St. Martin's Press   New York

Design by Judith A. Stagnitto

Library of Congress Cataloging-in-Publication Data

Kosoff, Susan.
      Good old-fashioned cookies / Susan Kosoff.
          p.   cm.
      ISBN 0-312-08801-9
      1. Cookies.   I. Title.
  TX772.K7   1993
  641.8′654—dc20   92-42132
                                CIP

First Edition: March 1993
10 9 8 7 6 5 4 3 2 1

For Mom, who knows a good cookie when she tastes one.
For Mark, who tastes only what he knows are good cookies.
For Jordan, who thinks all good cookies should be tasted!

Special thanks to my editor, Barbara Anderson, for her patience and helpful advice; to my good friend Sasha Rudenstein, for the use of her bedroom when writing at home became an impossible task; to Ellen Tucker and Jerry Raik, taste testers par excellence; to Lorna Vanterpool, for her extraordinary calm and devoted attention to my children, and for her expertise in the kitchen; to my husband, Paul, for taste-testing hundreds of cookies and not complaining when he gained weight; and to all the generous home bakers who shared their delicious recipes with me.

Contents

Introduction

Cookies are magical morsels. They can dry a child's tears, lift your spirits when you're down, and evoke an endless number of cherished memories—all with one bite. What's most amazing to me about homemade cookies is that you get not one, but *dozens* of these scrumptious treats—and you don't have to be a magician to make them!

Honestly, there's nothing mysterious or tricky about making old-fashioned cookies. When you know what to expect, baking becomes a quick and easy endeavor. The only surprise is the simplicity of your efforts.

If the idea of baking cookies conjures up hours of kitchen time in your mind, I have good news for you: Those days are over. Whether it's fragrant, crisp Snickerdoodles, spicy Ginger-Molasses Cookies, or Old-Fashioned Pinwheels, the following favorite recipes are intended to fill your cookie jar with a sentimental taste of times gone by, without taking hours of your time to prepare them.

All you need to do now is get started, bake, and enjoy!

Before You Begin

First things first: **Read through the entire recipe before you start to bake,** then get organized:

    1. Collect the necessary ingredients.   Chop nuts, beat eggs, and complete other small tasks before incorporating other ingredients.

    2. Bring butter, eggs, and other refrigerated ingredients to room temperature before mixing them together.   This takes about 30 minutes, but if you're pressed for time, grate the butter on a coarse grater, or cut it into small pieces and let stand at room temperature for 5 or 10 minutes before using. Place unshelled eggs in a bowl of hot tap water for 3 to 5 minutes to warm. Warm other dairy products in a saucepan over very low heat until tepid, or place the ingredient in a microwave-safe container and heat for about 20 seconds at high power.

    3. Preheat the oven fifteen minutes before you plan to bake the cookies.   Position the oven rack in the center of the oven for even baking. Use an oven thermometer.

    4. Grease cookie sheets only if the recipe directs you to do so. Spread a thin coat of solid vegetable shortening, unsalted butter, or margarine on cookie sheets with a pastry brush, butter wrapper, or small piece of paper towel. Some cookies spread too thin if baked on greased cookie sheets, so follow recipe directions carefully.

If you own only one cookie sheet, you can still bake large quantities of cookies. Simply line the cookie sheet with aluminum foil, grease if necessary, then fill with cookie dough and bake. In the meantime, for each cookie sheet you need, prepare additional sheets of aluminum foil with dough. When baked cookies are ready to come out of the oven, slide the foil onto a cooling rack and allow the cookies to cool on the foil. Next, carefully slide the hot cookie sheet under the next batch of cookies and *immediately* place it in the oven. Never place dough directly on a hot cookie sheet. The butter will melt too quickly, and your cookies will spread too thin and probably burn.

    5. Prepare a baking pan for brownies and other bar cookies. I like to bake bar cookies in a foil-lined pan because it's easier to lift out the baked layer in one piece. The layer can then be cut and served in neat, even pieces.

To line a pan with aluminum foil, tear off a sheet of foil approximately 6 inches longer than the size of the pan you want to line. Place foil, shiny side up, on the counter and center pan on foil. Lift and press foil, one side at a time, to conform to the outside of the pan (see illustration below). Remove the pan from foil and set aside on counter. Gently press the molded foil into the inside of the pan. Fold down the foil's two longer sides (after baking, they will be used as handles to lift out the baked layer of cookies). Lightly grease the bottom and sides of the prepared pan before spooning batter into it.

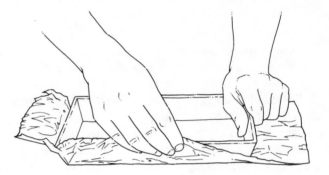

Ingredients and What They Do

For great-tasting cookies every time you bake, measure the ingredients carefully and use only the freshest, finest-quality ingredients available.

Main Ingredients

Baking powder.   This makes the cookie rise. An invention of the nineteenth century, baking powder is a chemical leavener that produces carbon dioxide gas. It's composed of an alkali substance (bicarbonate of soda) and an acid in the form of salt crystals (calcium acid phosphate). Originally, baking powder was "single acting," which means the chemical reaction (release of carbon dioxide gas) occurs as soon as the baking powder is mixed with the liquid in the dough. Today, the most commonly available baking powder is "double acting," composed of sodium aluminum sulfate–phosphate combinations. The chemical reaction process of double-acting baking powder is slower, allowing the gas release to occur twice—first when the powder is combined with liquid ingredients in the batter, and then again when the batter is placed in the hot oven. Always use *double-acting* baking powder for these recipes. If you're bothered by the slight aluminum aftertaste (most people can't detect it), bake with aluminum-free baking powder. You'll find it in some supermarkets and most health-food stores. Whatever type you choose, buy small quantities and use it within six months.

If you run out of baking powder, you can substitute ½ teaspoon cream of tartar *plus* ¼ teaspoon baking soda for each teaspoon of baking powder needed.

Baking soda.   Baking soda also makes the cookie rise. Baking soda (an alkali) is used as the leavening agent to balance the acid/alkali ratio when the cookie contains an acid ingredient such as buttermilk, sour cream, yogurt, or molasses. Mixed together, the acid and alkaline ingredients react chemically to produce the carbon dioxide gas and that makes the leavening occur. Baking soda works quickly and only once; there is no double action as there is in baking powder. Before you measure baking soda, stir it to eliminate any lumps, or shake it through a small, fine-meshed strainer.

Butter.   Butter contributes flavor, freshness, and texture. Use a top-quality, fresh, *unsalted* butter for these recipes. I use Land O Lakes for its superb flavor and solid fat content. *You can substitute unsalted margarine,* but don't expect the same cookie. Since margarine contains less fat and more water than butter, the shape, size, and, of course, the flavor of the cookies will be altered. *Salted butter or margarine* may be substituted as a last resort; but since salt acts as a preservative, it's often difficult to determine whether the butter is really fresh. If you use salted butter, omit the salt stated in the recipe.

Dough for refrigerator cookies or rolled-out cookies made with 100 percent corn oil margarine needs to be thoroughly chilled before baking. Chill refrigerator cookie dough for about 3 hours in the freezer, and dough for rolled-out cookies at least 5 hours. *Packaged whipped butter, soft margarine, or low-fat margarine spreads* will not work in these recipes. *Vegetable oil* may not be substituted for butter in these recipes.

Eggs. Eggs contribute liquid, flavor, color, and texture to your cookies. These recipes were tested using *large,* USDA-grade eggs. The color of the eggshell does not matter.

Flour. Use regular, bleached, all-purpose flour, unless otherwise indicated. *Unbleached flour* may be substituted for all-purpose flour, but *cake flour, self-rising, or instant-blending flour* will not work in these recipes.

Sugar and other sweeteners. Sugar contributes flavor to your cookies and helps brown them during baking. Most of these recipes call for *white, granulated sugar,* but *brown sugar* is used frequently, too. *Brown sugar* is processed sugar with molasses added to it. It's available in two forms: light and dark. (The dark has a more distinctive flavor.) When a recipe calls for brown sugar, you can use either light or dark, whichever you prefer or have on hand.

Confectioners' sugar is pulverized granulated sugar with added cornstarch, and is commonly known as powdered sugar or 10X sugar. It's used most often to decorate the tops of the cookies. Do not substitute confectioners' sugar for granulated or brown sugar in these recipes.

Honey, molasses, and corn syrup are liquid sweeteners used for their distinctive flavor. In a pinch, you can substitute one for another, but don't substitute other types of sugars for them or vice versa.

Other Ingredients

Chocolate. Use a good quality chocolate like Nestlé Toll-House when choosing semisweet or unsweetened chocolate. Some recipes call for *white baking bars or pieces.* Although white chocolate is not really chocolate, use brands containing cocoa butter for best flavor.

Unsweetened cocoa powder. Use real cocoa powder (such as Hershey's or Droste) and not a prepared, sweetened drink mix. To substitute cocoa for chocolate, use 3 level tablespoons of unsweetened cocoa plus 1 tablespoon soft butter, margarine, solid vegetable shortening, or bland cooking oil for each ounce of unsweetened chocolate needed.

Coconut.   Sweetened flaked or shredded coconut packaged in airtight bags or vacuum-sealed cans is fine to use in these recipes.

Dried fruits.   These include *apples, apricots, figs, dates, currants,* and dark and golden *raisins.* Always use dried fruits that are soft—hard fruit will not soften during baking.

To soften hard raisins, place them in a bowl with enough boiling water to cover. Soak the raisins about 10 minutes or until softened; pat dry before using.

To restore other hard, dried fruit, soak it briefly in boiling water just until tender. Drain and pat dry.

Extracts and other flavorings.   Vanilla and almond extracts add wonderful flavors to cookies. Always use pure extracts, never imitations. The cost is noticeably different, but so is the flavor.

Grated orange or lemon peel: Use freshly grated peel, or keep a stash, sealed airtight, in the freezer. To release the fullest flavor, beat peel into creamed butter and sugar for about 30 seconds before adding remaining ingredients.

To grate the peel: Choose fruit that is deep-colored, thick, and firm. Wash and dry fruit, then rub it across a small section of the grater, using short strokes. If you're using a four-sided grater, use the side with the smallest holes. Remove the peel with a stiff pastry brush or tap the grater several times against the work surface.

Food Coloring.   Use liquid or paste colors. Liquid colorings are sold in the baking section of most supermarkets. Paste colors are sold at cake-decorating-supply stores. Use paste colors sparingly since they are significantly more concentrated than liquid colors and yield deeper, more vivid colors.

Nuts.   As far as I'm concerned, fresh-tasting nuts are a welcome addition to almost any cookie. To keep nuts from turning rancid, store them in an airtight container in the refrigerator or freezer. Bring them to room temperature before adding to the dough, and always taste them just before using to make sure they're still fresh.

Peanut Butter.   Use chunky or smooth, but stick to the supermarket brands for these recipes. Freshly ground peanut butter, or health-food brands, may contain too much oil and alter the texture of the cookie.

Rolled Oats.   Use regular, uncooked old-fashioned oats or quick-cooking oats, never instant oatmeal.

Salt.   Most of these recipes use very little salt. You can omit it entirely, if necessary.

Equipment

Baking great-tasting cookies requires less time and energy when you own a few useful tools.

Cookie sheets and baking pans.   Use *shiny, heavyweight, aluminum* cookie sheets, never dark or flimsy sheets, which are more likely to burn the cookies during baking.

The best cookie sheets have a flat or barely turned-up edge, allowing hot air to reach every cookie from all directions. Also, to allow adequate air flow, use cookie sheets that are small enough to be at least 1 inch away from the oven walls on all sides.

Nonstick cookie sheets are useful, provided they are made from heavy-gauge metal and coated with a high-quality nonstick material or silicone resin. If you think the finish is worn or damaged, prepare the sheet according to the recipe directions. When removing cookies from nonstick sheets, use a wide rubber spatula that won't scratch the surface.

Insulated cookie sheets prevent cookies from burning on the bottom and promote even baking. Cookies baked on these double-layer insulated sheets, as a general rule, will require the maximum baking time given in the recipe.

Bake brownies and other bar cookies in shiny, heavyweight pans. Ovenproof glass pans can be substituted (be sure to use pans with the same dimensions called for in the recipe), but the oven temperature should be lowered by 25°F to prevent overbaking.

Chopstick.   No, this isn't a misprint. Keep a chopstick in the flour bin to stir the flour before measuring it into a dry cup. After spooning flour into the cup, use the chopstick to level off excess flour. Use it again to combine flour with other dry ingredients. No more sifting or table knife to wash!

Cookie cutters.   We have a drawerful in our house, including bears, bats, and bunnies. They're fun to use and collect, but jar lids, inverted cups, or drinking glasses are good substitutes when you need to cut round cookies but don't have a traditional cutter.

Double boiler.   A double boiler is two saucepans that fit together, one above the other. The bottom pan is filled one-third with water, and the top pan holds ingredients you want melted or cooked. If you don't own a double boiler, improvise by filling a two-quart saucepan one-third full with water, then set a smaller saucepan or heat-resistant mixing bowl snugly into the pan.

Electric mixer.   I use a heavy-duty, stationary stand mixer and paddle attachment when I make cookies, but a portable hand mixer will do the job just fine. Of course, if you have enough energy and the desire to exercise your arm, you can always mix the cookie dough the old-fashioned way.

Food processor.   Most cookie doughs can be mixed in a food processor. It won't aerate the butter as well as an electric mixer, but it will mix the dough in seconds. It's also good for chopping and grinding large amounts of nuts or dried fruits.

Measuring cups.   You need two types: one to measure liquids, the other to measure dry ingredients. Use a glass or plastic measuring cup with clear markings to measure fluid liquids such as milk, buttermilk, and juice. To measure dry ingredients you need a set of graduated measuring cups (¼ cup, ⅓ cup, ½ cup, and 1 cup) with flat rims. A 2-cup measure is handy to own, too. Use dry measuring cups to measure semisolid ingredients such as sour cream, yogurt, buttermilk, or mashed banana. Fill the cup to the rim and level with a knife.

Measuring spoons.   These are sold in graduated sets of ⅛ teaspoon, ¼ teaspoon, ½ teaspoon, 1 teaspoon, and 1 tablespoon. As far as I'm concerned, you can't own too many.

Oven thermometer.   Don't bake without it! A mercury oven thermometer ensures that your cookies are baking at the appropriate temperature. Use it every time you bake. Place thermometer in the center of the oven when you preheat, and wait 15 minutes before checking the temperature. If temperature is 50 degrees above or below the temperature you set, your oven needs to be calibrated. In the meantime, adjust the dial and wait until the correct temperature is recorded on the thermometer before putting the cookies in the oven.

Ice cream scoops (with lever, or squeeze handle).   These are not a necessity, but are useful to own since they take the guesswork out of measuring cookie batter. A scoop measuring 1¼ inches in diameter is roughly equivalent to 1 rounded teaspoon of dough. Use a 2-inch diameter scoop when a recipe calls for rounded tablespoons.

Ruler.   A ruler is a useful tool to keep in the kitchen drawer. Use it to measure uniform sized bar cookies, the thickness of a rolled-out dough, or the length, diameter, and thickness of a roll of refrigerator-cookie dough.

Sifters and sieves.   You don't have to sift flour for these recipes (page 6), so put away your sifter. Use a fine-meshed sieve to sift confectioners' sugar decoratively over cookies.

Spatulas and spoons.   Use a wide, metal pancake turner, or a long, narrow metal spatula to remove baked cookies from the cookie sheet. Large, flexible rubber spatulas make mixing and scraping cookie doughs a snap. If you're mixing the dough entirely by hand, you'll need a large wooden spoon to cream the butter and sugar. Most cookbooks advise using a wooden spoon to stir in chopped nuts, chocolate chips, and other additional ingredients, but I prefer using a large rubber spatula for those operations. Use *flatwear* teaspoons and tablespoons for measuring and dropping the dough.

Timer.   Cookies bake quickly and it's easy to forget they're in the oven. A minute timer helps you remember.

Wire cooling racks.   These may be purchased in any kitchenware store and are invaluable for cooling cookies after they have been removed from the oven.

Techniques: How to Bake a Perfect Batch of Cookies Every Time

Baking cookies from scratch is a snap when you know exactly what each term means.

Preparation Techniques

Beating.   Beating means to mix ingredients rapidly with the intent of forming and trapping air bubbles while at the same time producing a smooth mixture. An electric mixer does the job best.

Blending.   Blending means to mix ingredients together just until smooth and thoroughly combined. Use a large rubber spatula, wooden spoon, or the lowest setting on the electric mixer when you blend ingredients. Blending is different from beating because it's a slower, gentler motion. If you overmix the dough, the cookies will be tough.

Cream butter and sugar until light and smooth.   This means to beat softened butter and sugar together until pale in color, smooth, and light in texture. I use an electric mixer to cream butter and sugar, but hand-held beaters (either electric or manual) are good to use too. If you're creaming the old-fashioned way, mash the butter against the sides of the bowl with a wooden spoon until very soft and smooth. Add sugar, a few tablespoonfuls at a time, and work it into the butter until thoroughly blended.

Drop rounded teaspoonfuls (or tablespoonfuls) of dough onto greased cookie sheets.   For these recipes, use a *flatwear* teaspoon (not a measuring teaspoon) to measure equal amounts of dough. Use another spoon to push the dough portions onto the cookie sheet, spacing them according to the recipe directions.

An alternative to the teaspoon method is to use an ice cream scoop that has a lever or squeeze handle. The scoop will measure uniform portions of dough quickly and neatly and is available in several sizes. The one I use most often measures 1¼ inches in diameter and is roughly equivalent to a rounded teaspoonful of dough. For rounded tablespoonfuls of dough, use a scoop that measures 2 inches in diameter.

Measuring butter.   Each recipe calls for either cups or tablespoons of butter. One stick of butter is equivalent to ½ cup butter; 1½ sticks are equivalent to ¾ cups butter; and 2 sticks are equivalent to 1 cup butter. Each stick of butter is equivalent to eight tablespoons.

Measuring dry ingredients.   Use a set of standard, graduated measuring cups (page 7) to measure flour, sugar, oats, large amounts of cocoa, and other dry ingredients. Use graduated measuring spoons (page 7) to measure baking powder, baking soda, spices, cream of tartar, small amounts of cocoa powder, and other dry ingredients. Measure all ingredients carefully.

To measure flour: Stir the flour with a chopstick, wire whisk, or fork to aerate and remove any lumps. Place graduated measuring cup on counter and lightly spoon flour into cup until overflowing, then level top with chopstick or edge of a knife. Measure carefully, and don't pack, tap, or shake the measuring cup. Too much flour makes tough cookies!

To measure granulated sugar: Spoon or scoop sugar into graduated measuring cup and level with a metal spatula or the edge of a knife. If sugar is lumpy, break up lumps with your fingertips or push through a fine-meshed strainer before measuring.

To measure brown sugar: Dip graduated measuring cup into sugar and press sugar firmly into cup until sugar is level with the top edge. When accurately measured, sugar should hold the shape of the cup when turned out. Break up any hard clumps with your fingers before measuring.

To measure cocoa: Spoon unsifted cocoa into graduated measuring cup until overflowing, then level with edge of metal spatula or knife. If cocoa is hard and lumpy, stir or sift before measuring.

To measure confectioners' sugar. Measure as you would cocoa.

MEASUREMENTS USED MOST OFTEN

Pinch = amount you pick up between your thumb and forefinger
3 teaspoons = 1 tablespoon
4 tablespoons = ¼ cup
8 tablespoons = ½ cup
¼ cup butter = 4 tablespoons = ½ stick
⅓ cup butter = 5 ⅓ tablespoons (This measurement is a pet peeve of mine. When a recipe calls for ⅓ cup I measure 6 tablespoons of butter.)
½ cup butter = 8 tablespoons = 1 stick
¾ cup butter = 12 tablespoons = 1½ sticks
1 cup butter = 16 tablespoons = 2 sticks

Measuring liquid ingredients.   Use glass or plastic measuring cups with clear markings and a pouring spout. To measure accurately, put cup on a flat surface, bend down so that your eye is at cup level, and fill cup to correct mark.

10

Melting chocolate.   Chocolate burns easily when placed over direct heat. For best results, melt chocolate in the top part of a double boiler over barely simmering water. Be sure pan is dry before you add chocolate—it takes only one or two drops of water to tighten chocolate and prevent it from melting. If necessary, add ½ teaspoon *solid vegetable shortening* (not butter or oil) for every one ounce of chocolate, and stir until chocolate is smooth and glossy again.

To melt chocolate in a microwave oven, follow directions on the chocolate package or box.

Separating eggs.   Cold eggs are easier to separate, so separate them straight from the refrigerator. Tap the middle of one side of each egg firmly on the edge of a bowl to crack the shell. Using both hands, open shell at the crack and let some of the white run out into a clean bowl. Carefully guide the yolk back and forth between the two half shells, allowing the white to spill out completely. Drop yolk into another clean bowl. If a speck of yolk falls into the white, remove it with the tip of a cracked shell.

Sifting.   You don't have to sift flour for these recipes. Instead, aerate dry ingredients by stirring vigorously with a chopstick, wire whisk, or fork before measuring. If hard clumps of flour remain, sift the flour.

How to Measure or Shape
the Cookie Dough

The type of cookie dough you are working with will usually determine how the dough will be measured or shaped. Cookies are most often classifed into six groups: drop, bar, molded, refrigerator, pressed, and rolled. No matter what type of dough you are working with, strive to make all cookies on the cookies sheet the same size, shape, and thickness.

Drop cookies are made with a soft dough. Use a flatware teaspoon (not a measuring teaspoon) to measure dough. Use another spoon, or your fingers, to "drop" the dough onto cookie sheets.

Bar cookies are baked in a shallow pan, cooled, and cut into bars or squares. These are the easiest and quickest cookies to make because the dough is not measured or shaped.

Molded or hand-formed cookies are made by shaping firm dough into balls, crescents, and other shapes. To form balls, pinch off walnut-size pieces of dough and roll, one at a time, in the palms of your hands. Crescents are creating by rolling dough into balls then into small logs, then shaping the logs into half-moons. As always, strive to make cookies the same size and shape.

Refrigerator cookies are made from soft, creamy doughs that are shaped into logs and chilled until firm enough to slice. Unbaked logs may be frozen up to six weeks or refrigerated up to one week, if snugly wrapped.

11

To shape dough into a log, first divide the dough roughly in half. Transfer each half to a sheet of plastic wrap. Using plastic wrap and a rubber spatula as guides, lift and roll the dough into the dimensions stated in the recipe. Enclose the log snugly in plastic wrap. Place your palms at either end of the log and gently press to flatten and round out the ends (see illustration). Refrigerate or freeze the wrapped dough until firm enough to slice. When dough is firm, you can slice and bake it all at once, or only as needed.

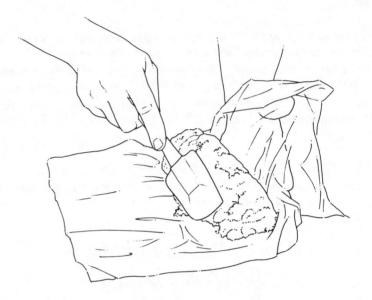

Pressed cookies are made with soft doughs that are forced through a cookie press to make decorative shapes. Depending on which template you choose, you can make pressed cookies in a variety of shapes and sizes. For best results, follow the manufacturer's directions for filling and using the press. If you don't own a cookie press, use a pastry bag with a shaped tip to squeeze out the dough.

Rolled cookies (cutouts) are made with a soft dough that usually requires chilling before shapes are cut out. Each recipe will tell you how long to chill the dough. If dough chills too long and becomes hard to roll out, let it sit on the counter for 5 or 10 minutes to soften. Before rolling dough, lightly flour work surface and rolling pin, or roll dough between two sheets of wax paper to prevent dough from sticking. To cut cookies, start at edge of dough and work towards center. Save scraps for re-rolling.

Baking Techniques

Make a "test run" before baking an entire batch.   It happens to all of us. You think you've followed a recipe faithfully, only to discover (after baking an entire sheet of cookies) that the cookies are ruined. Baking 2 or 3 cookies on a double thickness of aluminum foil allows you to see just how the cookies will bake and taste.

If cookies have spread too much, you may have to add a little more flour to the dough, or chill it until firm. If the cookie is too thick, try beating in a few tablespoons milk. Make another test run before baking the entire batch.

Place cookies correctly on the sheet.　Line cookies up in neat, even rows, leaving enough room for them to spread. Each recipe will tell you how far apart to space the cookies.

Bake one sheet at a time in the middle of the oven.　Cookies bake best when hot air circulates freely around them, and for that reason it's a good idea to bake them one sheet at a time. If your oven heats unevenly, turn the cookie sheet back to front halfway through baking time.

Use the correct size pan when baking bar cookies.　Scrape the batter into prepared pan, spreading it toward the sides and into corners with a rubber spatula. Smooth the surface. Bake on the middle rack in the center of the oven. *Note:* see "Substituting pan size" (page 17), if you don't have the size pan stated in the recipe.

Check the cookies to see if they're done.　It's often hard to tell when baking is complete. Some cookies are soft when they are ready to come out of the oven, others are crisp. Some cookies bake pale golden, others are brown around the edges. Each recipe will tell you how the cookies should look when they're done. Start checking the cookies 2 or 3 minutes before the end of the baking time stated; if cookies look done, take them out of the oven. If you're not certain, bake one or two minutes more and check again. Remember: A slightly underbaked cookie is always preferable to a burnt one.

Remove and cool cookies properly.　In general, cookies are removed with a metal spatula as soon as they are firm and easy to transfer. Follow recipe directions for removal, and don't let cookies sit on hot sheets longer than necessary. Cool cookies on wire racks, without crowding or stacking them, and wait until they are completely cooled before storing. When you bake cookies on aluminum foil, it's not necessary to remove cookies from the foil before cooling. Simply slide the foil onto a cooling rack and allow the cookies to cool on the foil.

Bar cookies are cooled in the pan on a wire rack, unless otherwise stated.

Final Touches

Decorated cookies are an extra-special treat, especially to children. For a quick treat, spread plain or colored icing over cooled cookies and top with sprinkles, colored sugars, chocolate chips, or raisins. For more elaborate lines, loops, dots, or doodles, use a pastry bag or a sturdy plastic bag to pipe the icing. Allow icing to harden before storing cookies.

To color the icing.   Divide icing into 3 or 4 small bowls, one for each color. Cover all but one bowl tightly with plastic wrap. Add 2 drops liquid food coloring to the uncovered bowl. Stir the coloring into the icing with a small rubber spatula. If you want a darker shade, add one more drop of coloring and stir it into the icing. If necessary, continue to add coloring one drop at a time, stirring after each addition, until you obtain the desired color. Cover the bowl tightly with plastic wrap. Wash and dry the spatula, and repeat the process to make other colors.

To use paste colors, dip the tip of a wooden toothpick into the paste, remove a tiny bit of the paste, and stir it into the icing to blend. Add more sparingly if you want a deeper color.

To pipe the icing.   Use a clean, dry piping bag and tip for each color of icing desired. If necessary, practice piping on a sheet of wax paper until you're satisfied with the results.

If you don't have a pastry bag, use a sturdy plastic food-storage bag for each color of icing. Spoon the icing into one corner of the bag and then twist the bag tightly closed above the icing (squeeze out the air as you twist the bag). Snip off a tiny piece of the corner just below the icing. Hold the bag at the twist with one hand, and use your other hand to press out the icing from the snipped corner. Practice piping on a sheet of wax paper, if necessary.

Cookie Cutting Guide

Bar cookies are usually cut into squares or rectangles, but diamond-and triangular-shaped cookies are an interesting addition to any cookie platter. To cut perfectly straight bar cookies, use a ruler to measure the size cookies you want, and then stick toothpicks in the cookie layer to mark where they should be cut. Lay the ruler across the top of the pan so that the edge of the ruler presses against one row of toothpicks. Pull a knife alongside the ruler and cut across the pan of cookies.

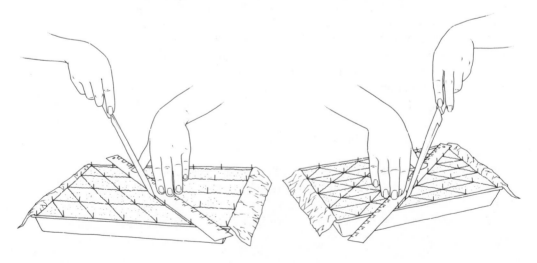

8- or 9-INCH SQUARE BAKING PAN*

NUMBER OF ROWS (length × width)	SIZE OF BAR	YIELD
4 × 4	2 inches × 2 inches	16
4 × 5	2 inches × 1½ inches	20
4 × 8	2 inches × 1 inch	32
5 × 5	1½ inches × 1½ inches	25
6 × 6	1¼ inches × 1¼ inches	36

11 × 7-INCH BAKING PAN

NUMBER OF ROWS (length × width)	SIZE OF BAR	YIELD
5 × 4	2¼ inches × 1¾ inches	20
5 × 5	2¼ inches × 1⅜ inches	25
8 × 4	1½ inches × 1¾ inches	32
8 × 5	1½ inches × 1⅜ inches	40
11 × 4	1 inch × 1¾ inches	44

9 × 13-INCH BAKING PAN

NUMBER OF ROWS (length x width)	SIZE OF BAR	YIELD
6 × 6	2⅛ inches × 1½ inches	36
8 × 5	1⅝ inches × 1¾ inches	40
8 × 6	1⅝ inches × 1½ inches	48
6 × 9	2 inches × 1 inch	54

15 × 10-INCH JELLY ROLL PAN

NUMBER OF ROWS (length × width)	SIZE OF BAR	YIELD
10 × 4	1½ inches × 2½ inches	40
12 × 4	1¼ inches × 2½ inches	48

* *Note:* A 9-inch square baking pan yields the same number of cookies, but each cookie will be slightly larger.

NUMBER OF ROWS	SIZE OF BAR	YIELD
(length × width)		
8 × 6	1¾ inches × 1¾ inches	48
10 × 5	1½ inches × 2 inches	50
9 × 6	1⅝ inches × 1⅝ inches	54
10 × 6	1½ inches × 1½ inches	60

Storing and Freezing Cookies

Before you even think about storing your cookies, make sure they are completely cooled. Always store crisp and soft cookies separately to maintain their individual textures. Store different varieties of cookies separately, too—you don't want your peanut butter cookies to taste like gingersnaps!

Most cookies will retain their oven-fresh taste and texture for up to one week, if stored in an airtight container. Storing airtight prevents moisture in the air from softening crisp cookies, and prevents soft cookies from drying out. Sealed plastic bags (with the air squeezed out before sealing), tins and plastic storage containers with tight-fitting lids, cookie jars, and glass jars with screw tops are good choices for storing cookies airtight.

Of course, if there are little (or big) cookie monsters at home who forget to close the container, storing cookies airtight may seem impossible. If necessary, you can *re-crisp cookies* by placing them on an ungreased cookie sheet in a 300°F oven for about 5 minutes. Transfer to a wire rack and cool before storing.

To soften dried-out cookies, add a piece of bread or an apple slice to the cookie container. Replace the apple often.

If you're storing cookies in the refrigerator, be sure to wrap airtight in plastic wrap to prevent strong odors from penetrating the cookies.

Bar cookies may be stored in an airtight container or tightly covered with foil or plastic wrap in the original baking pan.

Freezing baked cookies is a good idea if you want to keep them longer than a few weeks. Most cookies will stay fresh-tasting if wrapped airtight in a layer of plastic wrap and then a layer of aluminum foil. Packing them in an airtight container adds further protection against drying and freezer burn.

To defrost baked cookies, take them out of the container, unwrap them, and let them stand at room temperature for about 10 minutes.

A quick way to have freshly baked cookies on short notice is to freeze small portions of unbaked cookie dough in a double layer of plastic wrap and aluminum foil. Most doughs may be frozen for up to two months.

To defrost unbaked dough, unwrap and allow to soften at room temperature for about 30 minutes. Bake and enjoy!

Mailing Cookies

Mailing homemade cookies to friends and loved ones in faraway places is a sure way to make them smile. No need to wait for a special occasion, either—cookie gifts are a sign of affection and caring which most people would welcome anytime.

Selecting which cookies to mail.   Always choose sturdy cookies that stand the chance of surviving a bumpy journey. Never mail fragile cookies (Almond Lace Cookies, for example), or those with moist icings or frostings. In general, bar cookies, fruit cookies, drop, and molded cookies are usually the best travelers.

How to wrap, pack, and mail cookies.   There are several ways to package cookies for travel. You can wrap them in plastic or aluminum foil—either individually, in pairs, or in small stacks—or you can layer the cookies (with wax paper placed between layers) in sturdy, noncrushable plastic containers or decorative tins. Whichever method you choose, always put crumbled tissue paper or other filler on the bottom of the gift container to prevent the cookies from crushing. Pack cookies securely to prevent them from shifting, and place another layer of crumbled tissue on top of the cookies before closing the gift container.

You'll need a strong corrugated carton or packing box large enough to hold the gift container, as well as plenty of filler for insulation. Crumpled tissue paper or newspaper, styrofoam balls, plastic bubble-wrap, or popped corn all make fine fillers. To cushion the package of cookies, first place a thick layer of filler in the packing box. Set cookie package in the middle of the box and add as much filler as necessary around the sides of the package to prevent the cookies from being jostled. Bury the cookie container in another thick layer of filler before closing the box.

Seal the box with either nylon strapping tape or clear or brown reinforced packing tape. Don't use masking tape, plastic tape, or string. Mark "FRAGILE" in bold letters on front and back of the box. If possible, mail cookies first class on the day you bake them.

Substituting Ingredients and Pan Size

Substituting ingredients.   These recipes were written and tested using the ingredients listed, but don't be afraid to let your common sense guide you. For instance, substituting walnuts for pecans is never a matter for concern, but using baking soda in place of baking powder is quite another story. If you're not sure about a substitution, read the explanation for the ingredient you want substituted (pages 3–5) before making the change. If a substitution is recommended, it will say so. If not, *make no substitutions.*

Substituting pan size.   This is a little trickier, but not impossible. If you don't have the right size pan, you can substitute another pan with approximately the same or similar surface area (number of square inches) as the pan stated in the recipe. For instance, if a recipe specifies a 9-inch square pan (80 square inches), you can substitute an 8- by 10- by 2-inch oblong pan (80 square inches). Substituting pans with drastically different depths is not recommended.

Pans are measured across the top between the inside edges. Depending on the pan's size and shape, it may be necessary to adjust the baking time. Start testing at least 10 minutes before the indicated time.

ROUND CAKE PANS

8 × 1½ inches	50 square inches
9 × 1½ inches	64 square inches
8 × 2 inches	50 square inches
10 × 2 inches	79 square inches
12 × 2 inches	113 square inches

SQUARE AND RECTANGULAR CAKE PANS

9 × 9 × 1½ inches	81 square inches
11 × 7 × 1½ inches	77 square inches
13 × 9 × 2 inches	117 square inches
15 × 10 × 2 inches	150 square inches
15½ × 10½ × 1 inches	163 square inches

COOKIE BAKING BASICS

1. Read the recipe all the way through *before* you begin mixing the dough.

2. Use the freshest, finest quality ingredients available. Bring butter, eggs, and other chilled ingredients to room temperature (about 70°F) before using.

3. Preheat the oven for 10 to 15 minutes before baking the cookies. Use an oven thermometer to verify the temperature.

4. Grease the cookie sheet if stated in the recipe.

5. Measure all ingredients accurately. Use graduated dry measuring cups for dry ingredients and liquid measuring cups for liquids.

6. Avoid overmixing the dough after the dry ingredients have been added.

7. Try to make all cookies uniform in size, shape, and thickness. Follow the recipe directions for spacing the cookies, arranging them in even rows on the cookie sheet.

8. Place unbaked cookie dough on *completely cooled* cookie sheets. Warm cookie sheets will melt the butter in the dough, causing the cookies to spread and bake unevenly.

9. Bake cookies, one sheet at a time, on the middle rack. *Set the timer* as soon as you close the oven door.

10. Cool cookies completely before decorating or storing.

BAR COOKIE BASICS

Extra tips for baking the best-tasting, best-looking bar cookies every time you bake.

1. Use the exact size pan stated in the recipe.

2. For easy removal of baked cookies, line the baking pan with aluminum foil, allowing foil to overlap 2 inches beyond opposite sides of the pan. Lightly grease the bottom and sides of the foil-lined pan before adding batter.

3. For bar cookies with a crumb crust, use your fingers to spread the crust mixture in the baking pan and press it *evenly* into the bottom of the pan.

4. Bake bar cookies on the middle rack in the center of the oven.

5. Cool the cookie layer in the pan on a wire rack, unless otherwise stated.

6. Use the ends of the foil as handles to lift the cookie layer out of the pan before cutting it into bars or squares. If you've omitted the foil, remove a corner piece first, then remove remaining pieces.

Bar Cookies

Chocolate-Streaked Blondies

These chewy saucepan blondies are a snap to prepare.

6 tablespoons unsalted butter
1 cup firmly packed brown sugar
1 large egg, at room temperature
1 teaspoon vanilla extract
1 cup all-purpose flour

1 teaspoon baking powder
¼ teaspoon salt
½ chopped pecans
½ cup semisweet chocolate chips

COOKIE CUE

To keep brown sugar soft, store in an airtight container. To soften hard brown sugar, put sugar and a slice of soft bread in an airtight container. Within a few hours, the sugar will absorb the bread's moisture and soften.

1.   Position rack in center of oven; preheat oven to 350°F. Line an 8-inch square baking pan with aluminum foil, allowing foil to overlap 2 inches beyond opposite sides of pan. Lightly grease bottom and sides of prepared pan.

2.   In a heavy 2-quart saucepan over low heat, melt butter. Using a wooden spoon, stir in sugar and heat until mixture begins to bubble around edges. Remove pan from heat and cool 5 minutes.

3.   With a fork, beat egg and vanilla into butter mixture until blended. Add flour, baking powder, and salt, mixing with a rubber spatula until just blended. Stir in pecans and chocolate chips. Spread batter in prepared pan and smooth surface.

4.   Bake for 18 to 20 minutes, or until a toothpick inserted near center comes out clean. Remove pan to wire rack and cool completely. Use ends of foil to lift blondie layer out of pan, before cutting into bars or squares. Store bars in an airtight container.

Yield: 16 bars.

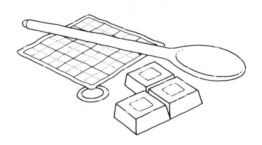

Cranberry-Nut Dream Bars

1¼ cups plus 2 tablespoons all-purpose flour, divided
1¼ cups plus 3 tablespoons granulated sugar, divided
½ cup cold, unsalted butter
1 cup finely chopped walnuts, divided into 2 ½-cup portions
2 large beaten eggs, at room temperature

2 tablespoons milk
1½ teaspoons vanilla extract
2 tablespoons finely grated orange peel
1 cup fresh or frozen and defrosted cranberries, coarsely chopped
½ cup flaked or shredded coconut
½ cup semisweet chocolate chips

1.   Position rack in center of oven; preheat oven to 350°F. Line a 13- by 9- by 2-inch baking pan with aluminum foil, allowing foil to overlap 2 inches beyond shorter sides of pan. Lightly grease bottom and sides of prepared pan.

2.   In a medium bowl, stir together 1¼ cups of the flour and the 3 tablespoons sugar. With a pastry blender, or two knives, cut butter into flour mixture until mixture resembles coarse crumbs. Stir in ½ cup of the chopped walnuts. With your fingers, spread mixture into prepared pan and press evenly into bottom. Bake for 15 minutes or until lightly browned.

3.   Meanwhile, in a large mixing bowl, and using a wire whisk or kitchen fork, combine the remaining 2 tablespoons flour and 1¼ cups sugar. Whisk in eggs, milk, vanilla, and orange peel until blended. Using a rubber spatula, fold in cranberries, coconut, and the remaining ½ cup chopped walnuts. Spread evenly over the hot, partially baked crust. Sprinkle chocolate chips over top.

4.   Bake again for 25 to 30 minutes or until surface is golden. Remove pan to wire rack and cool completely. Use ends of foil to lift cranberry-nut layer out of pan before cutting into bars or squares. Store bars in an airtight container in the refrigerator. These bars freeze well.

Yield: 36 bars.

Monkey Bars

Bananas and chocolate in a cakelike bar.

2¼ cups all-purpose flour
2 teaspoons baking powder
¼ teaspoon salt
½ cup unsalted butter, softened
⅓ cup granulated sugar
1 cup firmly packed brown sugar

2 large eggs, at room temperature
2 teaspoons vanilla extract
1 cup mashed, ripe bananas (about
    3 medium)
2 cups semisweet chocolate chips

COOKIE CUE

*Most bar cookies
are even more
delicious when
served with a scoop
of ice cream. Cut
brownies about
twice as large as the
recipe indicates
when serving with
ice cream.*

1.   Position rack in center of oven; preheat oven to 350°F. Line a 15- by 10-inch baking pan with aluminum foil, allowing foil to overlap 2 inches beyond shorter sides of pan. Lightly grease bottom and sides of prepared pan.

2.   In a small bowl, stir together flour, baking powder, and salt.

3.   In a large bowl, and using an electric mixer set on medium speed, cream butter, granulated sugar, and brown sugar until light and smooth. Beat in eggs, one at a time, until fluffy. Beat in vanilla. Add flour mixture alternately with banana, mixing with a rubber spatula after each addition. Stir in chocolate chips. Spread batter into prepared pan and smooth surface.

4.   Bake for 20 to 25 minutes, or until toothpick inserted in center comes out clean. Remove pan to wire rack and cool completely. Use ends of foil to lift banana-chocolate layer out of pan, before cutting into bars or squares. Store bars in an airtight container in the refrigerator.

Yield: 48 bars.

Lemon-Coconut Bars

If you're a lover of lemon meringue pie, this close cousin is sure to please.

Crust

1 cup unsalted butter, softened
½ cup confectioners' sugar

1 teaspoon vanilla extract
2 cups all-purpose flour

Lemon-Coconut Filling

4 large eggs, at room temperature
1¼ cups granulated sugar
⅓ cup fresh lemon juice
1 tablespoon finely grated lemon
   peel

Pinch salt
1½ cups sweetened flaked or
   shredded coconut

Topping

3 tablespoons confectioners' sugar

1.   Position rack in center of oven; preheat oven to 350°F. Line a 9- by 12-inch baking pan with aluminum foil, allowing foil to overlap 2 inches beyond shorter sides of pan. Lightly grease bottom and sides of prepared pan.

2.   *To prepare Crust:* In a large bowl, and using an electric mixer set on medium speed, cream butter and sugar until light and smooth. Beat in vanilla. Add flour in thirds, mixing with a rubber spatula after each addition. Spread evenly in prepared pan. Bake for 20 minutes, or until pale golden.

3.   *To prepare Lemon-Coconut Filling:* In a medium bowl, lightly beat together eggs, granulated sugar, lemon juice, lemon peel, and salt until blended. Stir in coconut. Pour lemon-coconut mixture over hot baked layer.

4.   Bake for 18 to 20 minutes longer, or until filling is set and lightly browned. Transfer pan to wire rack. Sift confectioners' sugar over hot filling to cover surface generously. Cool completely in pan on rack, and chill at least 4 hours before serving. Use ends of foil to lift lemon layer out of pan before cutting into bars or squares. Store bars in an airtight container in refrigerator.

Yield: 36 bars.

COOKIE CUE

Before squeezing a lemon, grate the peel and store in an airtight plastic bag for later use.

Cream Cheese Bars

This classic bar cookie has a crisp crust and a tart cream cheese filling.

Crust

1¼ cups all-purpose flour
½ cup firmly packed brown sugar

½ cup finely chopped walnuts
½ cup unsalted butter, softened

Cream Cheese Filling

1 8-ounce package cream cheese,
   softened
¼ cup granulated sugar
1 large egg, at room temperature

1 tablespoon fresh lemon juice
1 teaspoon vanilla extract

1.   Position rack in center of oven; preheat oven to 350°F. Line a 9-inch square baking pan with aluminum foil, allowing foil to overlap 2 inches beyond two opposite sides of pan. Lightly grease bottom and sides of prepared pan.

2.   *To prepare Crust:* In a medium bowl, stir together flour, brown sugar, and walnuts. Using a pastry blender or two knives, cut in butter until mixture resembles coarse crumbs. Remove ½ crumb mixture and set aside. With your fingers, press remaining mixture evenly into bottom of prepared pan. Bake for 15 minutes.

3.   *To prepare Cream Cheese Filling:* In a small bowl, and using an electric mixer set on medium speed, beat cream cheese until perfectly smooth, scraping the bowl often. Beat in sugar, egg, lemon juice, and vanilla until thoroughly blended. Pour cream cheese filling over hot, partially baked crust. Sprinkle with reserved crumb mixture.

4.   Bake for 25 minutes or until cream cheese filling is set. Remove pan to wire rack and cool completely. Use ends of foil to lift cream cheese layer out of pan before cutting into bars or squares. Store bars in an airtight container in the refrigerator.

Yield: 16 bars.

For **Cherry-Cheese Bars**: Omit lemon juice and vanilla extract and substitute ½ teaspoon almond extract. Bake cheese mixture for 10 minutes *without reserved crumb mixture.* Remove from oven and spoon one can (21-ounce) cherry pie filling over cheese. Sprinkle with reserved crumb mixture and bake for 15 to 20 minutes longer. Remove pan to wire rack and cool completely.

Yield: 16 bars.

COOKIE CUE

For the smoothest cream-cheese mixture, first soften cheese to room temperature and then beat on highest speed of electric mixer until very light and smooth, scraping sides and bottom of bowl often. Add additional ingredients only when you are certain there are no lumps remaining.

Marbled Cream Cheese Brownies

These moist, flavorful bars are made by swirling two batters together.

Cream Cheese Mixture

6 ounces cream cheese, softened
¼ cup granulated sugar
1 large egg, at room temperature

1 teaspoon vanilla extract
1 tablespoon flour

Brownie Mixture

¼ cup unsalted butter
4 squares semisweet chocolate
2 large eggs, at room temperature
⅔ cup granulated sugar
¼ teaspoon salt

1½ teaspoons vanilla extract
½ cup all-purpose flour
½ teaspoon baking powder
1 cup chopped pistachios, pecans,
  or walnuts

1.   *To prepare Cream Cheese Mixture:* In a small bowl, and using an electric mixer set on medium speed, beat cream cheese until perfectly smooth. Add sugar and beat for 2 minutes more. Beat in egg and vanilla until thoroughly blended. Beat in flour until blended.

2.   Position rack in center of oven; preheat oven to 350°F. Line an 8-inch square baking pan with aluminum foil, allowing foil to overlap 2 inches beyond opposite sides of pan. Lightly grease bottom and sides of prepared pan.

3.   *To prepare Brownie Mixture:* In a small, heavy pan over low heat, combine butter and chocolate, stirring constantly until melted and smooth. Set aside to cool.

4.   In a large bowl, and using an electric mixer set on high speed, beat eggs until very light in color. Gradually add sugar, beating well after each addition. Beat in salt and vanilla. On low speed, gradually beat in flour and baking powder until just blended. Blend in cooled chocolate mixture. Blend in chopped nuts.

5.   Using a rubber spatula, spread half of the Brownie Mixture in prepared pan. Pour Cream Cheese Mixture over top, spreading evenly to pan edges. Spoon remaining Brownie Mixture on top. Swirl a table knife through the layers of batter to create a marbled effect.

6.   Bake for 35 to 40 minutes, or until edges pull away from sides of pan and center of filling barely moves when pan is gently jiggled. Remove pan to wire rack and cool completely. Use ends of foil to lift cream-cheese brownie layer out of pan before cutting into bars or squares. Store bars in an airtight container in refrigerator.

Yield: 20 bars.

Glazed Chocolate Chip–
Peanut Butter Bars

Cookie Layer

½ cup unsalted butter, softened
¾ cup granulated sugar
⅓ cup firmly packed brown sugar
⅓ cup creamy peanut butter
1 large egg, at room temperature
1 teaspoon vanilla extract

1 cup all-purpose flour
¼ teaspoon baking soda
pinch salt
1 cup uncooked old-fashioned
 rolled oats
1 cup semisweet chocolate chips

Peanut Butter Glaze

⅓ cup confectioners' sugar
¼ cup creamy peanut butter

2 to 3 tablespoons milk

1.   Position rack in center of oven; preheat oven to 350°F. Line a 13- by 9-inch baking pan with aluminum foil, allowing foil to overlap 2 inches beyond shorter sides of pan. Lightly grease bottom and sides of prepared pan.

2.   *To prepare Cookie Layer:* In a large bowl, and using an electric mixer set on medium speed, cream butter and sugars until light and smooth. Beat in peanut butter until blended. Beat in egg and vanilla until fluffy.

3.   In a small bowl, stir together flour, baking soda, and salt. Add in thirds to creamed mixture, blending with a rubber spatula after each addition. Stir in oats. Spread batter into prepared pan and smooth surface.

4.   Bake for 22 to 27 minutes, or until no imprint remains when layer is lightly touched. Remove pan to wire rack and immediately sprinkle chocolate chips over hot surface. Wait 10 minutes for chips to soften before spreading them evenly over surface. Cool completely. Use ends of foil to lift peanut butter layer out of pan. Drizzle Peanut Butter Glaze over top. Allow glaze to harden before cutting into bars or squares. Store bars in an airtight container.

5.   *To prepare Peanut Butter Glaze:* In a small bowl, combine confectioners' sugar, peanut butter, and milk until smooth.

Yield: 48 bars.

Twice-Baked Cookies

Enjoy these crisp, hard cookies two ways—dipped into coffee, tea, milk, or wine, or straight from the cookie jar!

2 large eggs, at room temperature
1 cup granulated sugar
½ cup vegetable oil
½ teaspoon almond extract
1½ teaspoons vanilla extract
1 teaspoon grated orange peel
2½ cups all-purpose flour

1 teaspoon baking powder
¼ teaspoon baking soda
¼ teaspoon salt
1½ teaspoons anise seeds
1 cup golden raisins
1 cup unblanched whole almonds,
  coarsely chopped

1.   Position rack in center of oven; preheat oven to 350°F. Lightly grease and flour a cookie sheet.

2.   In a large bowl, and using an electric mixer set on high speed, beat eggs and sugar until thick and light in color, about 2 minutes. Slowly pour in oil, extracts, and orange peel and continue beating until mixture is thick and thoroughly blended, about 2 minutes.

3.   In another bowl, stir together flour, baking powder, baking soda, salt, anise seeds, raisins, and chopped almonds. On low speed, gradually beat flour mixture into egg mixture until dough is smooth and well blended. Scrape dough onto a lightly floured work surface. The dough should be soft but not sticky. If necessary, knead in up to ¼ cup more flour to form a soft, nonsticky dough.

4.   Divide dough in half. Shape each half into a 12- by 2-inch log. Place logs down the length of greased cookie sheet, spacing about 4 inches apart. Bake for 30 minutes, or until each log is firm and golden.

5.   Remove cookie sheet to wire rack and cool logs on sheet for 15 minutes. *Reduce oven temperature to 275°F.* Slide cooled logs onto a cutting board. Using a large, heavy chef's knife, cut logs, slightly on the diagonal, into ½-inch slices. The most efficient way to cut the logs is to place the tip of the knife on the board, then press down firmly, with one palm pressing on the dull side of the blade. This method allows you to cut through the almonds, and the cookies are less likely to crumble.

6.   Clean cookie sheet and then lightly grease. Arrange slices upright, spacing about ½ inch apart. Return slices to oven and bake 30 minutes more, or until lightly toasted. Transfer slices to wire rack and cool completely. Store cookies in an airtight container.

Yield: About 42 cookies.

Hermits

It's uncertain how this cookie got its name, but you can be sure that you won't be able to hide them once they've been tasted!

3¼ cups all-purpose flour
1 teaspoon ground cinnamon
1 teaspoon ground ginger
½ teaspoon ground nutmeg
½ teaspoon ground allspice
½ teaspoon salt
½ cup unsalted butter, softened
½ cup solid vegetable shortening

1¼ cups firmly packed brown
  sugar
2 large eggs, at room temperature
⅓ cup molasses
¼ teaspoon baking soda dissolved
  in ¼ cup warm water
1 cup chopped dried apricots
1 cup coarsely chopped walnuts

1.   In a large bowl, stir together flour, cinnamon, ginger, nutmeg, allspice, and salt.

2.   In another bowl, and using an electric mixer set on medium speed, cream butter, shortening, and sugar until light and smooth. Beat in eggs, one at a time, until fluffy. Blend in molasses. Add flour mixture alternately with dissolved baking soda, blending with a rubber spatula after each addition. Stir in apricots and walnuts.

3.   Position rack in center of oven; preheat oven to 350°F. Lightly grease 2 cookie sheets. Scrape approximately one fourth of the dough onto a sheet of plastic wrap. Using the plastic wrap and a rubber spatula as guides, shape dough into a 2-inch-wide, 1-inch-thick strip. Place strip down the length of greased cookie sheet. Repeat procedure with remaining dough. Each cookie sheet should contain two strips of dough, spaced about 2 inches apart.

4.   Bake one sheet at a time for 12 to 14 minutes, or until a toothpick inserted in the center of each strip comes out barely moist. Remove cookie sheet to wire rack and cool for 8 minutes. Using a metal spatula, slide warm strips onto a cutting board. Cut strips with a sharp knife, slightly on the diagonal, into 1½-inch bars. Transfer bars to wire racks and cool completely. Store bars in an airtight container.

Yield: Approximately 30 bars.

Chocolate Brownies and
Chocolate Cookies

Rocky Road Fudge Brownies

A blanket of marshmallows and nuts covers this classic brownie.

Fudge Brownies

1 cup unsalted butter
4 ounces unsweetened chocolate
4 large eggs, at room temperature
1¾ cups granulated sugar

2 teaspoons vanilla extract
1 cup all-purpose flour
¼ teaspoon baking powder

Rocky Road Frosting

4 ounces unsweetened chocolate
½ cup unsalted butter
½ cup heavy cream
1 tablespoon vanilla extract

3 cups confectioners' sugar
4 cups miniature marshmallows
1 cup chopped walnuts or pecans

COOKIE CUE

To test baking powder for freshness, add ½ teaspoon of the powder to ¼ cup hot water. If the water bubbles, the baking powder is fresh.

1. Position rack in center of oven; preheat oven to 350°F. Line a 13- by 9-inch baking pan with aluminum foil, allowing foil to overlap 2 inches beyond shorter sides of pan. Lightly grease bottom and sides of prepared pan.

2. *To prepare Fudge Brownies:* Put butter and chocolate in a small, heavy saucepan over low heat, stirring occasionally, until melted and smooth. Remove pan from heat and cool slightly.

3. In a large bowl, and using an electric mixer set on medium speed, beat eggs until frothy. Gradually add sugar, beating until mixture is thick. Beat in vanilla and cooled chocolate mixture until thoroughly blended.

4. In a small bowl, stir together flour and baking powder. Add in thirds to chocolate mixture, blending with a rubber spatula after each addition. Spread batter into prepared pan and smooth surface.

5. Bake for 25 to 30 minutes, or until a toothpick inserted in center comes out with several moist crumbs. Remove pan to wire rack and cool completely.

6. *To prepare Rocky Road Frosting:* In a small saucepan combine chocolate, butter, and heavy cream, stirring occasionally, until butter and chocolate melt. Scrape mixture into a large bowl and, with mixer set on medium speed, beat until smooth and thick. Beat in vanilla and confectioners' sugar until smooth. Stir in marshmallows and nuts.

7.   Spread Rocky Road Frosting over cooled brownies and chill several hours. Use ends of foil to lift brownie layer out of pan before cutting into bars or squares. Store bars in an airtight container in refrigerator.

Yield: 40 bars.

Cocoa Brownies

All chocolate lovers need at least one easy, but deliciously decadent, brownie recipe in their repertoire!

¾ cup unsalted butter, softened
½ cup unsweetened cocoa powder
1¼ cups granulated sugar
2 large eggs, at room temperature
1½ teaspoons vanilla extract

¼ teaspoon salt
⅓ cup sour cream
½ cup all-purpose flour
1 cup chopped walnuts or pecans
Confectioners' sugar

1.   Melt butter in a small, heavy saucepan over low heat. Remove pan from heat and whisk in cocoa until completely smooth. Cool slightly.

2.   Position rack in center of oven; preheat oven to 325°F. Line an 8-inch square baking pan with aluminum foil, allowing foil to overlap 2 inches beyond two opposite sides of pan. Lightly grease bottom and sides of prepared pan and dust with flour.

3.   In a large bowl, and using an electric mixer set on medium speed, beat together sugar, eggs, vanilla, and salt, until mixture is thick and light in color. On low speed, gradually beat cooled cocoa mixture into creamed mixture until blended. Blend in sour cream. Fold in flour with a rubber spatula. Fold in nuts. Spread batter into prepared pan and smooth surface.

4.   Bake for 25 to 30 minutes, or until a toothpick inserted near center comes out clean. Remove pan to wire rack and cool completely. Use ends of foil to lift brownie layer out of pan before cutting into bars or squares. Sift confectioners' sugar over bars before serving. Store bars in an airtight container at room temperature, or in the refrigerator or freezer.

Yield: 16 bars.

Applesauce Fudge Bars

If you like your brownies moist and fudgy, these bars are for you.

½ cup unsalted butter
2 ounces unsweetened chocolate
¾ cup granulated sugar
1 large egg plus 1 large egg white
   at room temperature
1 teaspoon vanilla extract

½ cup applesauce
¾ cup all-purpose flour
¼ teaspoon baking soda
1 cup chopped walnuts
Confectioners' sugar

1.   Melt butter and chocolate in a small, heavy saucepan over low heat, stirring constantly until smooth. Remove pan from heat and cool slightly.

2.   Position rack in center of oven; preheat oven to 350°F. Line a 9-inch square baking pan with aluminum foil, allowing foil to overlap 2 inches beyond two opposite sides of the pan. Lightly grease bottom and sides of prepared pan and dust with flour.

3.   In a large bowl, and using an electric mixer set on medium speed, beat together sugar, egg, egg white, and vanilla until mixture is thick, about 3 minutes. Beat in cooled chocolate mixture and applesauce until blended.

4.   In a small bowl, stir together flour and baking soda. On low speed, gradually beat flour mixture into chocolate mixture until just blended. Stir in walnuts. Using a rubber spatula, scrape batter into prepared pan and smooth surface.

5.   Bake for 15 to 20 minutes, or until a toothpick inserted near center comes out with a few moist crumbs. Remove pan to wire rack and cool completely. Use ends of foil to lift applesauce brownie layer out of pan before cutting into bars or squares. Sift confectioners' sugar over bars before serving. Store bars in an airtight container at room temperature, or in the refrigerator or freezer.

Yield: 12 bars.

Chocolate Dream Sandwich Cookies

Cookie Dough

½ cup unsalted butter, softened
¾ cup granulated sugar
2 large eggs, at room temperature
2 teaspoons vanilla extract

1½ cups all-purpose flour
½ cup cornstarch
⅓ cup unsweetened cocoa
Pinch salt

Vanilla Filling

½ cup unsalted butter, softened
2 cups confectioners' sugar
2 tablespoons corn syrup

½ teaspoon vanilla extract
Pinch salt

1.   *To prepare Cookie Dough:* In a large bowl, and using an electric mixer set on medium speed, cream butter and sugar until light and smooth. Beat in eggs and vanilla until fluffy.

2.   In a small bowl, stir together flour, cornstarch, cocoa, and salt. Add in thirds to creamed mixture, blending with a rubber spatula after each addition.

3.   Divide dough in fourths. Flatten each into a thick disk and wrap each disk snugly in plastic wrap. Chill 1 to 2 hours, or until firm enough to roll out. If dough is too firm to roll, unwrap and allow to soften at room temperature for 5 to 10 minutes.

4.   Position rack in center of oven; preheat oven to 350°F. Lightly grease 2 or 3 cookie sheets. Remove one disk of dough from refrigerator and roll out to ⅛-inch thickness. Cut dough with a 2-inch round cookie cutter. Lift up excess dough and save for re-rolling. Using a metal spatula, transfer cutouts to cookie sheets, spacing about 1 inch apart. Using a ¼-inch diameter thimble or pastry tip, cut a hole in the center of *half* the cutouts. If dough sticks to cutter, place cookie sheet in freezer for 5 minutes before trying again. Repeat procedure until all dough is used.

5.   Bake one sheet at a time for 10 to 12 minutes, or until cookies are firm. Using a metal spatula, slide cookies onto wire racks and cool completely.

6.   *To prepare Vanilla Filling:* Using an electric mixer, blender, or food processor, combine butter, confectioners' sugar, corn syrup, vanilla, and salt until smooth. Cover snugly with plastic wrap and set aside until needed.

7.   *To fill cookies:* Using a teaspoon of filling for each cookie, shape filling into a thick disk. Place disk on the underside of one cookie and press a holed cookie, underside down, on top. Repeat until all the cookies are filled. Store cookies in an airtight container.

Tint Hint: For gift-giving, tint the filling different colors. Divide filling equally into 3 or 4 small bowls and, leaving one filling white, tint the others pale pink, pale green, and pale yellow.

Yield: Approximately 40 cookies.

To prepare Vanilla Sandwich Cookies, omit cocoa and increase flour to 2 cups. **To prepare Chocolate Filling**, beat in 1 tablespoon unsweetened cocoa.

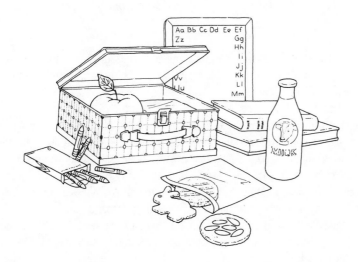

Chocolate Chip–Pecan Squares

Chewy, chunky, chocolate bars.

1 cup semisweet chocolate chips,
    divided into two ½-cup portions
3 tablespoons unsalted butter
⅓ cup dark corn syrup
¼ cup granulated sugar
1 cup chopped pecans

½ cup all-purpose flour
¼ teaspoon salt
2 large eggs, at room temperature
1 tablespoon rum (optional)
Confectioners' sugar

1.   Put ½ cup of the chocolate chips, butter, corn syrup, and granulated sugar in a small, heavy saucepan over low heat, and stir constantly until smooth. Remove pan from heat and cool slightly.

2.   Position rack in center of oven; preheat oven to 325°F. Line an 8-inch square baking pan with aluminum foil, allowing foil to overlap 2 inches beyond two opposite sides of pan. Lightly grease bottom and sides of prepared pan and dust with flour.

3.   In a small bowl, stir together pecans, flour, salt, and remaining ½ cup chocolate chips. In another bowl, lightly beat together eggs and rum. Stir egg mixture into cooled chocolate mixture. Stir pecan mixture into chocolate-egg mixture. Spread batter into prepared pan and smooth surface with a rubber spatula.

4.   Bake for 25 to 30 minutes, or until a toothpick inserted near center comes out with a few moist crumbs. Remove pan to wire rack and cool completely. Use ends of foil to lift chocolate-pecan layer out of pan, before cutting into squares or bars. Sift confectioners' sugar over squares before serving. Store squares in an airtight container at room temperature, or in the refrigerator or freezer.

Yield: 16 squares.

Chocolate Crinkles

2 tablespoons unsalted butter
2 ounces unsweetened chocolate
1 cup all-purpose flour
¾ teaspoon baking powder
¼ teaspoon salt

½ cup granulated sugar
2 large eggs, at room temperature
½ teaspoon vanilla extract
Confectioners' sugar

1.   Put butter and chocolate in top part of a double boiler over barely simmering water. When ingredients soften, remove pan from water and stir until smooth. Cool slightly.

2.   In a large bowl, and using an electric mixer set on low speed, whisk together flour, baking powder, salt, and granulated sugar. Beat in eggs, vanilla, and cooled chocolate mixture until smooth and blended. Cover and chill 1 hour, or until dough is firm and easy to handle.

3.   Position rack in center of oven; preheat oven to 350°F. Lightly grease 2 or 3 cookie sheets. Spread enough confectioners' sugar to cover bottom of a shallow pan.

4.   Pinch off pieces of dough and roll, one at a time, into 1¼-inch round balls. Roll six or seven balls at a time in confectioners' sugar to coat completely. Arrange balls on greased cookie sheets, spacing about 1½ inches apart.

5.   Bake one sheet at a time for 8 minutes, or until cookies crack and feel firm when gently pressed. Using a metal spatula, slide cookies onto wire racks and cool completely. Store cookies in an airtight container.

Yield: Approximately 30 cookies.

Chocolate-Covered Coconut Kisses

½ cup sweetened condensed milk
1 teaspoon vanilla extract
⅛ teaspoon salt
2¾ cups sweetened shredded
   coconut

½ cup finely chopped almonds
2 cups semisweet chocolate chips

1.   Position rack in center of oven; preheat oven to 350°F. Lightly grease 1 large cookie sheet.

2.   In a large bowl, whisk together condensed milk, vanilla, and salt. Add coconut and chopped almonds and stir until well mixed.

3.   Drop scant tablespoonfuls of dough onto greased cookie sheet, spacing about 1 inch apart. With your fingers, shape cookies into mounds about 1½ inches high. Bake for 13 to 15 minutes, or until each cookie is pale golden. Using a metal spatula, slide cookies onto wire racks and cool completely.

4.   Meanwhile, in top part of a double boiler over barely simmering water, melt chocolate until smooth. Spear cooled coconut kisses, one at a time, on a fork and dip into chocolate to cover completely. Shake gently to remove excess chocolate before placing on waxed paper or aluminum foil. Allow chocolate to harden at room temperature before storing cookies. Store cookies in an airtight container.

Yield: Approximately 24 cookies.

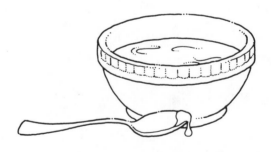

Devil's Food Cookies

Serve these cookies with a tall glass of milk.

¼ cup buttermilk
2 ounces unsweetened chocolate
½ cup firmly packed brown sugar
1 teaspoon vanilla extract
½ cup unsalted butter, softened
¾ cup granulated sugar

1 large egg, at room temperature
2 cups all-purpose flour
½ teaspoon baking powder
½ teaspoon baking soda
¼ teaspoon salt
½ cup sprinkles (any flavor)

1.   Put buttermilk, unsweetened chocolate, and brown sugar in a small, heavy saucepan. Cook over low heat, stirring occasionally with a wooden spoon, until melted and smooth. Remove pan from heat and stir in vanilla extract. Cool slightly.

2.   Position rack in center of oven; preheat oven to 350°F. Lightly grease 2 or 3 cookie sheets.

3.   In a large bowl, and using an electric mixer set on medium speed, cream butter and granulated sugar until light and smooth. Beat in egg until fluffy. Beat in cooled chocolate mixture until blended.

4.   In a small bowl, stir together flour, baking powder, baking soda, and salt. Add in thirds to chocolate mixture, blending with a rubber spatula after each addition. Stir in sprinkles.

5.   Drop rounded teaspoonfuls of dough onto greased cookie sheets, spacing about 2 inches apart. Bake one sheet at a time for 8 to 10 minutes, or until cookies feel firm. Remove cookie sheet to wire rack and cool 2 minutes. Using a metal spatula, slide cookies onto wire racks and cool completely. Store cookies in an airtight container.

Yield: Approximately 45 cookies.

Drop Cookies

Banana–Chocolate Chip Nut Drops

½ cup unsalted butter, softened
½ cup granulated sugar
½ cup firmly packed brown sugar
1 large egg, at room temperature
½ teaspoon vanilla extract
1 cup very ripe, mashed banana
  (about 3 medium bananas)

1⅓ cups all-purpose flour
½ teaspoon baking soda
¼ teaspoon salt
⅛ teaspoon nutmeg
1½ cups semisweet chocolate chips
1 cup coarsely chopped walnuts

1.   Position rack in center of oven; preheat oven to 375°F. Lightly grease 2 or 3 cookie sheets.

2.   In a large bowl, and using an electric mixer set on medium speed, cream butter and sugars until light and smooth. Beat in egg and vanilla until fluffy. Stir in banana.

3.   In a small bowl, stir together flour, baking soda, salt, and nutmeg. Add in thirds to creamed mixture, blending with a rubber spatula after each addition. Stir in chocolate chips and chopped walnuts.

4.   Drop rounded teaspoonfuls of dough onto greased cookie sheets, spacing about 2 inches apart. Bake one sheet at a time for 8 to 10 minutes or until edges are lightly browned. Remove cookie sheet to wire rack and cool 2 minutes. Using a metal spatula, slide cookies onto wire racks and cool completely. Store cookies in an airtight container.

Yield: Approximately 48 cookies.

Oatmeal Jumbles

These cookies are large and chewy.

½ cup unsalted butter, softened
½ cup granulated sugar
⅓ cup firmly packed brown sugar
2 large eggs, at room temperature
1 teaspoon vanilla extract
1 cup all-purpose flour
1 teaspoon baking soda

¼ teaspoon salt
1 cup uncooked old-fashioned
    rolled oats
1½ cups raisins
1 cup coarsely chopped pecans
1 cup semisweet chocolate chips

COOKIE CUE

To test whether eggs are fresh, put them in a bowl of cold, salted water. If they stay at the bottom of the bowl, they're fresh.

1.   Position rack in center of oven; preheat oven to 375°F. Have ready 2 or 3 ungreased cookie sheets.

2.   In a large bowl, and using an electric mixer set on medium speed, cream butter and sugars until light and smooth. Beat in eggs and vanilla until fluffy.

3.   In a small bowl, stir together flour, baking soda, and salt. Add in thirds to creamed mixture, blending with a rubber spatula after each addition. Stir in oats, raisins, pecans, and chocolate chips.

4.   Drop rounded tablespoonfuls of dough onto ungreased cookie sheets, spacing about 2 inches apart. Bake one sheet at a time for 10 to 12 minutes, or until cookies are lightly browned and tops look dry. Using a metal spatula, slide cookies onto wire racks and cool completely. Store cookies in an airtight container.

Yield: Approximately 30 cookies.

Frosted Pineapple-Date Cookies

These cakelike cookies are not too sweet.

Cookies

1 8-ounce can crushed pineapple
  in its own juice
½ cup unsalted butter, softened
¾ cup firmly packed brown sugar
½ cup granulated sugar
1 large egg, at room temperature

½ cup plain yogurt
2½ cups all-purpose flour
½ teaspoon baking soda
Pinch salt
1 cup snipped dates

Pineapple–Cream Cheese Icing

2 tablespoons cream cheese, at
  room temperature
2 tablespoons unsalted butter

2 tablespoons reserved pineapple
  juice
1⅓ cups confectioners' sugar

1.　Set a mesh strainer in a medium bowl and pour in pineapple and its juice. Using the back of a tablespoon, press pineapple to extract as much extra juice as possible. Remove pineapple and put in a double layer of paper towel and pat until very dry. Reserve juice in bowl.

2.　Position rack in center of oven; preheat oven to 350°F. Lightly grease 2 or 3 cookie sheets.

3.　In a large bowl, and using an electric mixer set on medium speed, cream butter and sugars until light and smooth. Beat in egg, yogurt, and pineapple until blended.

4.　In a small bowl, stir together flour, baking soda, and salt. On low speed, gradually beat flour mixture into creamed mixture until thoroughly blended. Stir in dates.

5.　Drop rounded teaspoonfuls of dough onto greased cookie sheets, spacing about 2 inches apart. Bake one sheet at a time for 12 to 15 minutes or until cookie edges are browned. Using a metal spatula, slide cookies onto wire racks and cool completely.

6.　*To prepare Pineapple–Cream Cheese Icing:* In a medium bowl, beat together cream cheese, butter, and 2 tablespoons reserved pineapple juice until smooth and fluffy. Gradually beat in confectioners' sugar until blended. Spread icing over cooled cookies. Allow icing to dry before storing cookies. Store cookies between sheets of wax paper in an airtight container.

Yield: Approximately 52 cookies.

COOKIE CUE

To prevent sticking, dip scissors or knife into water each time you cut dried fruit.

Ranger Cookies

Millie Kennedy, of Madison, Wisconsin, contributed this popular, well-known recipe. Over the last thirty years, she has gently refined it, but it remains a "family favorite" to this day.

½ cup unsalted butter, softened
½ cup granulated sugar
⅓ cup firmly packed brown sugar
1 large egg, at room temperature
1 teaspoon vanilla extract
1 cup all-purpose flour
½ teaspoon baking soda

¼ teaspoon baking powder
⅛ teaspoon salt
1 cup uncooked old-fashioned
    rolled oats
1¼ cups crispy rice cereal, such as
    Rice Krispies
½ cup sweetened flaked coconut

1. Position rack in center of oven; preheat oven to 375°F. Lightly grease 2 or 3 cookie sheets.

2. In a large bowl, and using an electric mixer set on medium speed, cream butter and sugars until light and smooth. Beat in egg and vanilla until fluffy.

3. In a small bowl, stir together flour, baking soda, baking powder, and salt. Add in thirds to creamed mixture, blending with a rubber spatula after each addition. Stir in oats, rice cereal, and coconut.

4. Drop rounded teaspoonfuls of dough onto greased cookie sheets, spacing about 2 inches apart. Bake one sheet at a time for 8 to 10 minutes, or until cookies are pale golden. Using a metal spatula, slide cookies onto wire racks and cool completely. Store cookies in an airtight container.

Yield: Approximately 40 cookies.

Classic Chocolate Chip Cookies

1 cup unsalted butter, softened
¾ cup granulated sugar
¾ cup firmly packed brown sugar
2 large eggs, at room temperature
1 teaspoon vanilla extract
½ teaspoon water

2¼ cups all-purpose flour
1 teaspoon baking soda
1 teaspoon salt
2 cups semisweet chocolate chips
1 cup coarsely chopped walnuts

1. Position rack in center of oven; preheat oven to 375°F. Lightly grease 2 or 3 cookie sheets.

2. In a large bowl, and using an electric mixer set on medium speed, cream butter and sugars until light and smooth. Beat in eggs, vanilla, and water until fluffy.

3. In a small bowl, stir together flour, baking soda, and salt. Add in thirds to creamed mixture, blending with a rubber spatula after each addition. Stir in chocolate chips and chopped walnuts.

4. Drop rounded teaspoonfuls of dough onto greased cookie sheets, spacing about 2 inches apart. Bake one sheet at a time for 8 to 10 minutes or until edges are lightly browned. Using a metal spatula, slide cookies onto wire racks and cool completely. Store cookies in an airtight container.

Yield: Approximately 48 cookies.

Orange–Chocolate Chip Cookies

Orange and chocolate are a choice combination in this crisp cookie.

½ cup unsalted butter, softened
⅓ cup granulated sugar
⅓ cup firmly packed light brown
  sugar
2 teaspoons finely grated orange
  peel

1 large egg, at room temperature
1¼ cups all-purpose flour
½ teaspoon baking soda
¼ teaspoon salt
¾ cup semisweet chocolate chips
½ cup chopped walnuts

━ ⌣ ⌣ ━
C O O K I E   C U E

*Keep a plastic bag
in the vegetable
shortening can and
use like a mitten
when greasing pans
and cookie sheets.*

1.   Position rack in center of oven; preheat oven to 375°F. Lightly grease 3 or 4 cookies sheets.

2.   In a large bowl, and using an electric mixer set on medium speed, cream butter and sugars until light and smooth. Beat in orange peel. Beat in egg until fluffy.

3.   In a small bowl, stir together flour, baking soda, and salt. Add in thirds to creamed mixture, blending with a rubber spatula after each addition. Stir in chocolate chips and walnuts.

4.   Drop rounded teaspoonfuls of dough onto greased cookie sheets, spacing about 2 inches apart. Bake one sheet at a time for 10 to 12 minutes, or until cookies are lightly browned. Using a metal spatula, slide cookies onto wire racks and cool completely. Store cookies in an airtight container.

Yield: Approximately 48 cookies.

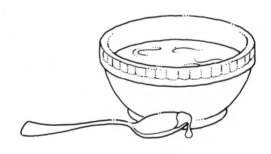

Coconut Crisps

1 cup sweetened flaked or
　shredded coconut
½ cup unsalted butter, softened
½ cup granulated sugar
2 teaspoons finely grated lemon
　peel

1 large egg, at room temperature
1 teaspoon vanilla extract
1 tablespoon fresh lemon juice
1⅓ cups all-purpose flour
½ teaspoon baking soda
¼ teaspoon salt

1.　Position rack in center of oven; preheat oven to 375°F. Lightly grease 2 or 3 cookie sheets.

2.　In the container of a food processor fitted with a steel blade, process coconut, butter, and sugar until smooth and creamy. Add lemon peel and process for 30 seconds. Add egg, vanilla, and lemon juice and process until thoroughly blended.

3.　In a small bowl, stir together flour, baking soda, and salt. Gradually add flour mixture to butter mixture, processing until just blended.

4.　Drop level tablespoonfuls of dough onto greased cookie sheet, spacing about 2 inches apart. Bake one sheet at a time for 9 to 11 minutes, or until cookie edges are lightly browned and tops feel firm when touched. Using a metal spatula, slide cookies onto wire racks and cool completely. Store cookies in an airtight container.

Yield: Approximately 40 cookies.

Chocolate Chunk–Buttermilk Cookies

Buttermilk and egg white help reduce the fat in these tender, cakelike cookies.

1¾ cups all-purpose flour
1 teaspoon baking soda
¼ teaspoon salt
¼ cup unsalted butter, softened
½ cup granulated sugar
¼ cup firmly packed brown sugar

1 large egg, plus 1 large egg white
1½ teaspoons vanilla extract
⅓ cup buttermilk, at room temperature
6 ounces semisweet chocolate, cut into ½-inch chunks

1.   Position rack in center of oven; preheat oven to 375°F. Lightly grease 2 or 3 cookie sheets.

2.   In a small bowl, stir together flour, baking soda, and salt.

3.   In a large bowl, and using an electric mixer set on medium speed, cream butter and sugars until light and smooth. Beat in egg, egg white, and vanilla until fluffy. On low speed, add flour mixture alternately with buttermilk, blending well after each addition. Stir in chocolate chunks.

4.   Drop rounded tablespoonfuls of dough onto greased cookie sheets, spacing about 2 inches apart. Bake 10 to 12 minutes, or until edges are lightly browned. Using a metal spatula, slide cookies onto wire racks and cool completely. Store cookies in an airtight container.

Yield: Approximately 24 cookies.

Old-Fashioned Raisin-Oatmeal Cookies

These old-fashioned favorites are crisp on the outside, chewy and moist on the inside.

½ cup unsalted butter, softened
½ cup granulated sugar
⅓ cup firmly packed brown sugar
2 large eggs, at room temperature
2 tablespoons milk or water
1 teaspoon vanilla extract
1 cup all-purpose flour

1 teaspoon baking soda
½ teaspoon ground cinnamon
¼ teaspoon salt
1½ cups uncooked old-fashioned
  rolled oats
1½ cups raisins

1.   Position rack in center of oven; preheat oven to 375°F. Grease 2 or 3 cookie sheets.

2.   In a large bowl, and using an electric mixer set on medium speed, cream butter and sugars until light and smooth. Beat in eggs, milk, and vanilla until fluffy.

3.   In a small bowl, stir together flour, baking soda, cinnamon, and salt. Add in thirds to creamed mixture, blending with a rubber spatula after each addition. Stir in oats and raisins.

4.   Drop rounded tablespoonfuls of dough onto greased cookie sheets, spacing about 2 inches apart. Bake one sheet at a time for 12 to 15 minutes, or until edges are lightly browned and tops feel firm when touched. Using a metal spatula, slide cookies onto wire racks and cool completely. Store cookies in an airtight container.

Yield: Approximately 36 cookies.

Chocolate Chip–Raisin Drops

These soft, plump cookies have a hint of nutmeg.

½ cup unsalted butter, softened
¾ cup granulated sugar
1 large egg, plus 1 large egg
   white, at room temperature
1 teaspoon vanilla extract
1 8-ounce container vanilla yogurt

1¾ cups all-purpose flour
½ teaspoon baking soda
¼ teaspoon salt
½ teaspoon ground nutmeg
1 cup semisweet chocolate chips
1½ cups dark raisins

1.   Position rack in center of oven; preheat oven to 350°F. Lightly grease 2 or 3 cookie sheets.

2.   In a large bowl, and using an electric mixer set on medium speed, cream butter and sugar until light and smooth. Beat in egg, egg white, and vanilla. Blend in yogurt and don't worry if mixture curdles.

3.   In a small bowl, stir together flour, baking soda, salt, and nutmeg. Add in thirds to creamed mixture, blending with a rubber spatula after each addition. Stir in chocolate chips and raisins.

4.   Drop rounded teaspoonfuls of dough onto greased cookie sheets, spacing about 2 inches apart. Bake one sheet at a time for 8 to 10 minutes, or until edges are lightly browned. Remove cookie sheet to wire rack and cool for 2 minutes. Using a metal spatula, slide cookies onto wire racks and cool completely. Store cookies in an airtight container.

Yield: Approximately 46 cookies.

Iced Apple Drop Cookies

Don't bother to peel the apples for these soft, flavorful cookies.

½ cup unsalted butter, softened
1⅓ cups firmly packed brown
  sugar
1 large egg, at room temperature
¼ cup milk
2 cups all-purpose flour
1 cup uncooked old-fashioned
  rolled oats
1 teaspoon baking soda

1 teaspoon ground cinnamon
½ teaspoon ground nutmeg
¼ teaspoon salt
1 cup diced, unpeeled apple
  (1 medium apple)
½ cup chopped walnuts
1 cup chopped raisins
Vanilla Icing (page 110)

1. Position rack in center of oven; preheat oven to 375°F. Lightly grease 2 or 3 cookie sheets.

2. In a large bowl, and using an electric mixer set on medium speed, cream butter and sugar until light and smooth. Beat in egg and milk until fluffy.

3. In a small bowl, stir together flour, oats, baking soda, cinnamon, nutmeg, and salt. Add in thirds to creamed mixture, blending with a rubber spatula after each addition. Stir in apple, walnuts, and raisins.

4. Drop rounded teaspoonfuls of dough onto greased cookie sheets, spacing about 2 inches apart. Bake one sheet at a time for 9 to 11 minutes or until cookies are lightly browned. Using a metal spatula, slide cookies onto wire racks and cool completely. Dip a fork into Vanilla Icing and drizzle over cookies in thin lines. Let icing harden before storing cookies. Store cookies in an airtight container.

Yield: Approximately 45 cookies.

COOKIE CUE

Decorate cookies with homemade colored sugar. Stir 2 or 3 drops food coloring into 2 tablespoons granulated sugar until desired color is obtained.

Macadamia Nut–Raisin Cookies

This is one of my favorite cookies. They're plump but crisp, and chock full of nuts, raisins, and chips.

½ cup unsalted butter, softened
½ cup granulated sugar
¼ cup firmly packed brown sugar
1 large egg, at room temperature
1 teaspoon vanilla extract
1¼ cups all-purpose flour

1 teaspoon baking soda
¼ teaspoon salt
1 3½-ounce jar macadamia nuts,
  coarsely chopped
1¼ cups raisins
1 cup semisweet chocolate chips

1. Position rack in center of oven; preheat oven to 350°F. Lightly grease 2 or 3 cookie sheets.

2. In a large bowl, and using an electric mixer set on medium speed, cream butter and sugars until light and smooth. Beat in egg and vanilla until fluffy.

3. In another bowl, stir together flour, baking soda, and salt. Add in thirds to creamed mixture, blending with a rubber spatula after each addition. Stir in macadamia nuts, raisins, and chocolate chips until well combined.

4. Drop rounded tablespoonfuls of dough onto greased cookie sheets, spacing about 2 inches apart. Bake one sheet at a time for 12 to 14 minutes, or until cookies are lightly browned.

5. Remove cookie sheet to wire rack and cool for 2 minutes. Using a metal spatula, slide cookies onto wire racks and cool completely. Store cookies in an airtight container.

Yield: Approximately 30 cookies.

Lorna's Lemon Rock Cookies

Lorna Vanterpool first baked these cookies with her mother more than forty years ago. It's a tender, flavorful cookie you can count on when you want to bake something quickly.

¾ cup unsalted butter, softened
¾ cup granulated sugar
1½ teaspoons lemon peel
2 large eggs, at room temperature

2 cups all-purpose flour
⅓ cup currants or chopped dark
*   raisins*

1. Position rack in center of oven; preheat oven to 350°F. Lightly grease 2 or 3 cookie sheets.
2. In a large bowl, and using an electric mixer set on medium speed, cream butter and sugar until light and smooth. Beat in lemon peel, about 30 seconds. Beat in eggs until fluffy. Add flour in thirds, blending with a rubber spatula after each addition. Stir in currants or raisins.
3. Drop rounded teaspoonfuls of dough onto greased cookie sheets, spacing about 1 inch apart. Bake one sheet at a time for 8 to 10 minutes, or until cookies are pale golden and firm. Using a metal spatula, slide cookies onto wire racks and cool completely. Store cookies in an airtight container.

Yield: Approximately 54 cookies.

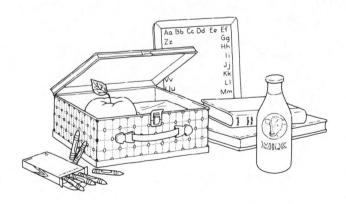

Soft Pumpkin Cookies

Similar to Rock Cookies in appearance and texture, these cookies are spicy and packed with pumpkin flavor.

½ cup unsalted butter, softened
1¼ cups firmly packed brown
   sugar
1 large egg, at room temperature
1 teaspoon vanilla extract
1 cup canned pumpkin
1¼ cups all-purpose flour
½ teaspoon baking powder

½ teaspoon baking soda
1 teaspoon ground cinnamon
¾ teaspoon ground nutmeg
1 cup toasted wheat germ
¾ cup chopped walnuts
½ cup raisins
Vanilla Icing (page 110)

1.   Position rack in center of oven; preheat oven to 375°F. Lightly grease 2 or 3 cookie sheets.

2.   In a large bowl, and using an electric mixer set on medium speed, cream butter and sugar until light and smooth. Beat in egg and vanilla until fluffy. Add pumpkin a few tablespoons at a time, and beat until thoroughly blended.

3.   In a small bowl, stir together flour, baking powder, baking soda, cinnamon, and nutmeg. Add in thirds to creamed mixture, blending with a rubber spatula after each addition. Stir in wheat germ, walnuts, and raisins.

4.   Drop rounded teaspoonfuls of dough onto greased cookie sheets, spacing about 2 inches apart. Bake one sheet at a time for 8 to 10 minutes, or until edges are firm. Using a metal spatula, slide cookies onto wire racks and cool completely. Spread Vanilla Icing over tops of cookies with a small spatula. Allow glaze to harden. Store cookies in an airtight container.

Yield: Approximately 46 cookies.

Ice Cream Sandwiches

These chocolate chip–oatmeal cookies are also delicious without the ice cream filling.

¾ cup unsalted butter, softened
¾ cup granulated sugar
½ cup firmly packed brown sugar
1 tablespoon vegetable oil
1 large egg, at room temperature
2 tablespoons water
2 teaspoons vanilla extract
1¼ cups all-purpose flour
¼ cup unsweetened cocoa powder

1 teaspoon baking soda
¼ teaspoon salt
3 cups uncooked quick-cooking
  rolled oats
2 cups semisweet chocolate chips
1 quart (approximately) ice cream
  (your favorite flavor, of course!),
  softened

1. In a large bowl, and using an electric mixer set on medium speed, beat together butter, sugars, and oil until light and smooth. Beat in egg, water, and vanilla until blended.

2. In a small bowl, stir together flour, cocoa, baking soda, and salt. Add in thirds to creamed mixture, blending on low speed after each addition. Stir in rolled oats and chocolate chips.

3. Position rack in center of oven; preheat oven to 350°F. Line 2 or 3 cookie sheets with aluminum foil; lightly grease foil.

4. Pinch off pieces of dough and roll, one at a time, into 2¼-inch balls. Arrange balls on foil-lined cookie sheets, spacing about 3 inches apart. Bake one sheet at a time for 10 to 13 minutes, or until edges of cookies are firm and tops look almost dry. Do not overbake. Transfer cookie sheet to a wire rack and cool for about 1 minute. Gently slide cookies with foil liner onto wire racks and cool completely.

5. To assemble sandwiches, spread approximately ½ cup softened ice cream on bottom of one cookie. Place a second cookie, bottom side facing down, on top of ice cream. Wrap each sandwich snugly in plastic wrap and freeze for at least 2 hours, or until firm.

Yield: 12 ice cream sandwiches.

Note: Soften ice cream in refrigerator 20 to 30 minutes before using.

Molded, Rolled, and Refrigerator Cookies

Walnut Crescents

Cookie Dough

1 cup unsalted butter, softened
½ cup confectioners' sugar
2 teaspoons vanilla extract
Pinch salt

1¾ cups all-purpose flour
½ teaspoon cinnamon
1 cup finely chopped walnuts

Cinnamon Sugar

½ cup granulated sugar
1 teaspoon cinnamon

1. *To prepare Cookie Dough:* In a large bowl, and using an electric mixer set on medium speed, cream butter and sugar until light and smooth. Beat in vanilla and salt until blended.

2. In a small bowl, stir together flour and cinnamon. Add in thirds to creamed mixture, blending with a rubber spatula after each addition. Stir in walnuts. Shape dough into a ball, flatten into a thick disk, and wrap snugly in plastic wrap. Chill dough 2 hours, or until firm.

3. *To prepare Cinnamon Sugar:* Put sugar and cinnamon in a shallow baking dish and shake pan gently until evenly blended.

4. Position rack in center of oven; preheat oven to 325°F. Have ready 2 or 3 ungreased cookie sheets.

5. Pinch off pieces of dough and roll, one at a time, into 1-inch balls. Roll each ball into a log, about 3 inches long by ½ inch thick. Form each log into a crescent shape and place on ungreased cookie sheets, spacing about 1 inch apart.

6. Bake one sheet at a time for 15 to 18 minutes or until cookies are firm. Do not let cookies brown. Using a metal spatula, slide cookies onto wire racks. Roll warm cookies in Cinnamon Sugar to coat completely. Cool cookies on wire racks. Store cookies in an airtight container.

Yield: Approximately 60 cookies.

COOKIE CUE

Cool and clean cookie sheets before baking each batch of cookies. Hot sheets will melt butter in dough, causing cookies to spread too quickly.

Basic Scottish Shortbread

¼ *cup confectioners' sugar*
1¼ *cups all-purpose flour*

½ *cup unsalted butter, softened
and cut into 8 pieces*

1. Position rack in center of oven; preheat oven to 300°F.
2. In a large bowl, stir together sugar and flour. Scatter butter over flour mixture. Using your fingertips, work butter into flour mixture until dough holds together to form a ball. Dust work surface with flour and knead dough a few minutes until smooth and soft.
3. Pat dough into an ungreased 8-inch round cake pan. Using a kitchen fork, press ¾-inch lines all around perimeter of dough. Prick surface of dough all over with fork tines.
4. Bake for 40 to 45 minutes or until edges are barely golden. Do not allow shortbread to brown. Remove pan to wire rack and cool for 10 minutes. Invert pan on wire rack and let shortbread drop out. Flip shortbread right side up and transfer to cutting board. While still warm, cut shortbread with a large, heavy chef's knife into 12 to 16 pie-shaped wedges. Transfer wedges to wire racks and cool completely. Store wedges in an airtight container.

Yield: 12 to 16 wedges.

Snickerdoodles

A simple but yummy old-fashioned favorite.

Cinnamon-Sugar Topping

3 tablespoons granulated sugar
2 teaspoons ground cinnamon

Cookie Dough

½ cup unsalted butter, softened
⅔ cup granulated sugar
1 large egg, at room temperature
½ teaspoon vanilla extract

1⅓ cups all-purpose flour
½ teaspoon baking soda
½ teaspoon cream of tartar
⅛ teaspoon salt

1.   Position rack in center of oven; preheat oven to 375°F. Lightly grease 2 or 3 cookie sheets.

2.   *To prepare Cinnamon-Sugar Topping:* Put sugar and cinnamon in a shallow baking pan, and shake pan gently until evenly blended.

3.   *To Prepare Cookie Dough:* In a large bowl, and using an electric mixer set on medium speed, cream butter and sugar until light and smooth. Beat in egg and vanilla until fluffy.

4.   In a small bowl, stir together flour, baking soda, cream of tartar, and salt. Add in thirds to creamed mixture, blending with a rubber spatula after each addition. Drop rounded tablespoonfuls of dough, a few at a time, into Cinnamon-Sugar Topping. Roll cookies to cover completely, shaping them into balls as you roll.

5.   Arrange balls on greased cookies sheets, spacing about 2 inches apart. Flatten each ball slightly with the bottom of a drinking glass.

6.   Bake one sheet at a time for 8 to 10 minutes, or until edges are golden brown. Using a metal spatula, slide cookies onto wire racks and cool completely. Store cookies in an airtight container.

Yield: Approximately 32 cookies.

Classic Peanut-Butter Cookies

A cookie-jar favorite with the traditional crisscrossed top.

½ cup unsalted butter, softened
½ cup firmly packed brown sugar
½ cup peanut butter
1 large egg, at room temperature

½ teaspoon vanilla extract
1¾ cups all-purpose flour
½ teaspoon baking soda

COOKIE CUE

Store flour in a clean, airtight container in a cool, dry place to maintain maximum freshness.

1. Position rack in center of oven; preheat oven to 350°F. Lightly grease 2 or 3 cookie sheets.

2. In a large bowl, and using an electric mixer set on medium speed, cream butter and sugar until light and smooth. Gradually beat in peanut butter, egg, and vanilla until fluffy.

3. In a small bowl, stir together flour and baking soda. Add in thirds to creamed mixture, blending with a rubber spatula after each addition.

4. Pinch off pieces of dough and roll, one at a time, into 1-inch balls. Arrange balls on greased cookie sheets, about 2 inches apart. Flatten each ball with a floured fork to make crisscross pattern.

5. Bake one sheet at a time for 10 to 12 minutes, or until cookies are lightly browned. Remove cookie sheet to wire rack and cool for 1 minute. Using a metal spatula, slide cookies onto wire racks and cool completely. Store cookies in an airtight container.

Yield: Approximately 40 cookies.

Orange–Coconut Crisp Cookies

½ cup unsalted butter, softened
¾ cup plus 3 tablespoons
   granulated sugar, divided
1 tablespoon finely grated orange
   peel
1 large egg yolk
1 tablespoon milk

1 teaspoon vanilla extract
1½ cups all-purpose flour
¼ teaspoon baking soda
¼ teaspoon baking powder
¼ teaspoon salt
1½ cups sweetened shredded or
   flaked coconut

1.   Position rack in center of oven; preheat oven to 375°F. Lightly grease 2 or 3 cookie sheets.

2.   In a large bowl, and using an electric mixer set on medium speed, cream butter and the ¾ cup sugar until light and smooth. Beat in orange peel. Beat in egg yolk, milk, and vanilla until blended.

3.   In a small bowl, stir together flour, baking soda, baking powder, and salt. Add in thirds to creamed mixture, blending with a rubber spatula after each addition. Stir in coconut.

4.   Pinch off pieces of dough and roll, one at a time, into 1½-inch balls. Arrange balls on greased cookie sheets, spacing about 2 inches apart. Dip bottom of a drinking glass into remaining 3 tablespoons sugar and then use the glass to flatten each cookie to ¼-inch thickness.

5.   Bake one sheet at a time for 9 to 11 minutes, or until cookie edges are brown and tops feel firm when touched. Remove cookie sheet to wire rack and cool for 2 minutes. Using a metal spatula, slide cookies onto wire racks and cool completely. Store cookies in an airtight container.

Yield: Approximately 24 cookies.

Melting Moments

This tender, fragile cookie lives up to its name.

1 cup unsalted butter, softened
½ cup confectioners' sugar
1 teaspoon vanilla extract
1¼ cups all-purpose flour

¾ cup cornstarch
Pinch salt
Confectioners' sugar

1. In a large bowl, and using an electric mixer set on medium speed, cream butter and the ½ cup confectioners' sugar until light and smooth. Beat in vanilla.

2. In a small bowl, stir together flour, cornstarch, and salt. Add in thirds to creamed mixture, blending with a rubber spatula after each addition. Transfer dough to a sheet of plastic wrap, flatten into a thick disk, and wrap snugly. Chill for 1 hour, or until dough is easy to handle.

3. Position rack in center of oven; preheat oven to 350°F. Have ready 2 or 3 ungreased cookie sheets. Pinch off pieces of dough and roll, one at a time, into 1¼-inch balls. Arrange balls on ungreased cookie sheets, spacing about 2 inches apart.

4. Bake one sheet at a time for 12 to 15 minutes or until cookie edges begin to brown. Remove cookie sheet to wire rack and cool for 3 or 4 minutes. Using a metal spatula, transfer 6 or 7 cookies to a shallow baking pan and generously sift confectioners' sugar over cookies to coat completely. Transfer cookies to wire racks and cool completely. Repeat until all cookies have been coated. Sift additional confectioners' sugar over cookies before serving. Store cookies in an airtight container.

Yield: Approximately 45 cookies.

Lacy Almond-Oat Cookies

Crisp and sweet, lace cookies are characterized by their large holes. Be sure to leave plenty of space for the cookies to spread.

½ cup unsalted butter, softened
1 cup firmly packed brown sugar
1 teaspoon vanilla extract
½ teaspoon cinnamon
1¼ cups uncooked old-fashioned
 oats

½ cup finely chopped (not ground)
 almonds
½ cup all-purpose flour
2 squares semisweet chocolate

1.   Position rack in center of oven; preheat oven to 350°F. Line 2 or 3 cookie sheets with aluminum foil.

2.   In a large bowl, and using an electric mixer set on medium speed, beat together butter, sugar, vanilla, cinnamon, oats, almonds, and flour until thoroughly combined.

3.   Pinch off pieces of dough and roll, one at a time, into 1-inch balls. Arrange balls on prepared cookie sheets, spacing about 3 inches apart.

4.   Bake one sheet at a time for 7 to 9 minutes, or until cookies are lacy and golden. Cookies will look soft. Transfer cookie sheet to wire rack and cool for 5 minutes. Slide foil onto a wire rack and cool cookies completely.

5.   Melt chocolate in top part of a double boiler over barely simmering water. Dip a teaspoon into melted chocolate and with it drizzle thin lines over cookies. Let chocolate harden before storing cookies. Remove cookies from foil with a metal spatula. Store cookies in an airtight container.

Yield: Approximately 48 cookies.

COOKIE CUE

If you want your oatmeal cookies to have a nuttier flavor, place a single layer of oats in a large roasting pan and toast in a 300°F oven for 8 to 10 minutes, or until barely golden.

Plump Ginger-Molasses Cookies

These large, old-fashioned cookies fill your kitchen with a wonderful aroma while baking.

½ cup unsalted butter, softened
¾ cup firmly packed brown sugar
¼ cup molasses
1 tablespoon water
1 large egg, at room temperature
1½ cups all-purpose flour

¾ teaspoon baking soda
¾ teaspoon ground cinnamon
½ teaspoon ground cloves
1 teaspoon ground ginger
⅛ teaspoon salt

COOKIE CUE

Molasses will slip out of a measuring cup easily if you lightly oil the cup before adding the molasses.

1. Position rack in center of oven; preheat oven to 350°F. Lightly grease 1 or 2 cookie sheets.

2. In a large bowl, and using an electric mixer set on medium speed, beat butter, sugar, molasses, and water until light and smooth. Beat in egg until fluffy.

3. In a small bowl, stir together flour, baking soda, cinnamon, cloves, ginger, and salt. Add in thirds to creamed mixture, blending with a rubber spatula after each addition.

4. Pinch off pieces of dough and roll, one at a time, into 1½-inch balls. Arrange balls on greased cookie sheets, spacing about 2 inches apart.

5. Bake one sheet at a time for 15 minutes, or until cookies are puffed and feel firm when lightly touched. Using a metal spatula, slide cookies onto wire racks and cool completely. Store cookies in an airtight container.

Yield: Approximately 24 cookies.

Gingersnaps

Crisp and thin, these cookies really snap!

6 tablespoons unsalted butter,
   softened
⅓ cup firmly packed brown sugar
¼ cup honey or corn syrup
¼ cup molasses
2 cups all-purpose flour

2 teaspoons baking soda
2 teaspoons ground ginger
½ teaspoon ground cinnamon
½ teaspoon ground cloves
¼ teaspoon ground allspice

1.   Put butter, sugar, honey or syrup, and molasses in a heavy, 2-quart saucepan over low heat, and stir until smooth and blended. Scrape mixture into a large bowl and cool slightly.

2.   Position rack in center of oven; preheat oven to 350°F. Lightly grease 2 or 3 cookie sheets.

3.   In a small bowl, stir together flour, baking soda, ginger, cinnamon, cloves, and allspice. Using a large wooden spoon, gradually stir flour mixture into cooled butter mixture, blending well after each addition. The dough should be soft, but easy to handle. If necessary, chill dough in the freezer about 5 minutes before proceeding with the next step.

4.   Pinch off pieces of dough and roll, one at a time, into 1¼-inch balls. Arrange balls on greased cookie sheets, spacing about 3 inches apart.

5.   Bake one sheet at a time for 13 to 15 minutes, or until cookies are firm and slightly cracked. Remove cookie sheet to wire rack and cool for 2 minutes. Using a metal spatula, slide cookies onto wire racks and cool completely. Store cookies in an airtight container.

Yield: Approximately 45 cookies.

Old-Fashioned Pinwheel Cookies

This is a simple refrigerator dough, made fancy by a few extra steps.

1 ounce unsweetened chocolate
1⅓ cups all-purpose flour
1¼ teaspoons baking powder
¼ teaspoon salt
2 tablespoons milk

1½ teaspoons vanilla extract
½ cup unsalted butter, softened
½ cup granulated sugar
1 large egg yolk

1.   Put chocolate in top part of a double boiler over barely simmering water. When chocolate softens, remove pan from water and stir until smooth. Cool slightly.

2.   In a small bowl, stir together flour, baking powder, and salt.

3.   Measure milk in a liquid measuring cup, and stir in vanilla.

4.   In a large bowl, and using an electric mixer set on medium speed, cream butter and sugar until light and smooth. Beat in egg yolk until blended. On low speed, add flour mixture alternately with milk mixture, blending well after each addition.

5.   Remove half the dough, flatten into a thick rectangle, and wrap snugly in plastic wrap. Stir cooled chocolate into remaining dough. Remove chocolate dough and repeat procedure as with vanilla dough. Chill both doughs about 2 hours, or until firm enough to roll out. If dough is too firm to roll, unwrap and allow to soften at room temperature for 5 to 10 minutes.

6.   Roll out chocolate dough between 2 sheets of plastic wrap into a 12- by 8-inch rectangle. Remove top sheet of plastic from dough. Repeat procedure with vanilla dough. Invert chocolate dough on top of vanilla dough and remove plastic from chocolate dough. Using plastic wrap on bottom of vanilla dough and a spatula as guides, roll doughs tightly together, jelly-roll fashion, starting with longer side. Cut roll in half to make two 6-inch rolls. Wrap each roll snugly in plastic wrap and chill 3 hours, or until firm enough to slice.

7.   Position rack in center of oven; preheat oven to 350°F. Have ready 2 or 3 ungreased cookie sheets. Cut dough into ¼-inch thick slices. Arrange slices on ungreased cookie sheets, spacing about 1 inch apart.

8.   Bake one sheet at a time for 8 to 10 minutes, or until cookies feel firm when lightly touched. Using a metal spatula, slide cookies onto wire racks and cool completely. Store cookies in an airtight container.

Yield: Approximately 48 cookies.

Raisin-Oatmeal Refrigerator Cookies

This crisp, spicy cookie is a big favorite around my house

½ cup unsalted butter, softened
½ cup vegetable shortening
1 cup firmly packed brown sugar
1 large egg, at room temperature
1 teaspoon vanilla extract
1¾ cups all-purpose flour
¼ teaspoon salt

½ teaspoon baking soda
½ teaspoon ground cinnamon
⅛ teaspoon ground cloves
1 cup uncooked quick-cooking
   rolled oats
1 cup golden raisins

1. In a large bowl, and using an electric mixer set on medium speed, cream butter, shortening, and sugar until light and smooth. Beat in egg and vanilla until fluffy.

2. In a small bowl, stir together flour, salt, baking soda, cinnamon, and cloves. Add in thirds to creamed mixture, blending with a rubber spatula after each addition. Stir in oats and raisins.

3. Divide dough in half and transfer each half to a sheet of plastic wrap. Using the wrap and a rubber spatula as guides, shape each half into an 8- by 2-inch log. Wrap logs snugly and chill 3 hours, or until firm enough to slice.

4. Position rack in center of oven; preheat oven to 375°F. Have ready 3 or 4 ungreased cookie sheets. Cut logs into ¼-inch thick slices. Arrange slices on ungreased cookie sheets, spacing about 1 inch apart.

5. Bake one sheet at a time for 7 to 9 minutes or until cookie edges are lightly browned. Remove cookie sheet to wire rack and cool 1 minute. Using a metal spatula, slide cookies onto wire racks and cool completely. Store cookies in an airtight container.

Yield: Approximately 60 cookies.

COOKIE CUE

Refrigerator cookies can be made in half an hour of spare time and chilled until needed. You can slice and bake all at once, or only as needed.

Peanut-Butter and White-Chocolate Cookies

The addition of white chocolate makes this cookie irresistible.

6 tablespoons unsalted butter,
   softened
1/2 cup granulated sugar
1/4 cup peanut butter
1 large egg, at room temperature
1/2 cup all-purpose flour

1/3 cup unsweetened cocoa powder
1/2 teaspoon baking powder
1/4 teaspoon baking soda
1/8 teaspoon salt
1 3-ounce bar white chocolate, cut
   into 1/4-inch pieces

1.   In a large bowl, and using an electric mixer set on medium speed, cream butter and sugar until light and smooth. Beat in peanut butter until blended. Beat in egg until fluffy.

2.   In a small bowl, stir together flour, cocoa powder, baking powder, baking soda, and salt. Add in thirds to creamed mixture, blending with a rubber spatula after each addition. Stir in white chocolate pieces.

3.   Divide dough in half and transfer each half to a sheet of plastic wrap. Using the wrap and a rubber spatula as guides, shape each half into a 4½-inch by 2-inch log. Wrap logs snugly in plastic wrap and chill 2 hours, or until firm enough to slice.

4.   Position rack in center of oven; preheat over to 350°F. Have ready 2 or 3 ungreased cookie sheets. Using a heavy chef's knife, cut logs into 1/4-inch thick slices. Arrange slices on ungreased cookie sheets, spacing about 2 inches apart.

5.   Bake one sheet at a time for 10 to 12 minutes, or until cookies are firm to the touch. Do not overbake. Using a metal spatula, slide cookies onto wire racks and cool completely. Store cookies in an airtight container.

Yield: Approximately 24 cookies.

Lemon Cream-Filled Cookies

Cookie Dough

½ cup unsalted butter, softened
½ cup granulated sugar
2 large egg yolks, at room
temperature
1 tablespoon milk
1 tablespoon finely grated lemon
peel

1½ teaspoons vanilla extract
2 cups all-purpose flour
1 teaspoon baking powder
½ teaspoon salt

Filling

2 tablespoons unsalted butter,
softened
1 cup confectioners' sugar

1 teaspoon finely grated lemon
peel
2 tablespoons fresh lemon juice

1. *To prepare Cookie Dough:* In a large bowl and using an electric mixer set on medium speed, cream butter and sugar until light and smooth. Beat in egg yolks, milk, lemon peel, and vanilla until blended.

2. In a small bowl, stir together flour, baking powder and salt. Add in thirds to creamed mixture, blending at low speed after each addition. After the third addition of flour, dough is ready when it begins to hold together.

3. Divide dough in half and transfer each half to a sheet of plastic wrap. Using the wrap and a rubber spatula as guides, shape each half into an 8- by 1½-inch log. Wrap logs snugly and chill 2 hours, or until firm enough to slice.

4. Position rack in center of oven; preheat oven to 375°F. Have ready 2 or 3 ungreased cookie sheets. Cut logs into ⅛-inch slices. Arrange slices on ungreased cookie sheets, spacing about 1 inch apart.

5. Bake one sheet at a time for 10 to 12 minutes, or until cookie edges begin to brown lightly. Using a metal spatula, slide cookies onto wire racks and cool completely.

6. *To prepare Filling:* In a small bowl, beat together butter, confectioners' sugar, lemon peel, and lemon juice until smooth. Cover until needed.

7. Spread 1 teaspoon filling on undersides of half the cookies. Top with remaining cookies, undersides down. Store cookies in an airtight container.

Yield Approximately 48 cookies.

Traditional Butter Cookies

──── ⌇ ⌇ ────

COOKIE CUE

*To prevent dough
from sticking, dip
cutting edge of
cookie cutter into
flour before pressing
into rolled-out
dough. To cut the
cookies, press cookie
cutter firmly into
dough until it
touches the work
surface. Wiggle the
cutter slightly to
loosen from dough,
then lift up the
cutter to remove
entirely.*

──── ⌇ ⌇ ────

COOKIE CUE

*Design your own
cookie pattern. On
cardboard, draw
desired shape or
trace pictures from
magazines. Cut out
cardboard outline.
Lightly grease one
side of cardboard
before placing,
greased side down,
on dough. Use a
small sharp knife to
cut around edges of
cardboard. Remove
cardboard and
transfer cutout to
cookie sheet.
Regrease cardboard,
if necessary, before
each use.*

¾ cup unsalted butter, softened
⅔ cup granulated sugar
2 teaspoons grated lemon peel
1 large egg, at room temperature

1¼ teaspoons vanilla extract
¼ teaspoon salt
2¼ cups all-purpose flour

1. In a large bowl, and using an electric mixer set on medium speed, cream butter and sugar until light and smooth. Beat in lemon peel, about 30 seconds. Beat in egg, vanilla, and salt until fluffy. Add flour in thirds, blending on low speed after each addition.

2. Divide dough into fourths. Transfer each dough portion to a sheet of plastic wrap, flatten into a thick disk, and wrap snugly. Chill 1 hour, or until firm enough to roll out. If dough is too firm, unwrap and allow to soften at room temperature for 5 to 10 minutes.

3. Position rack in center of oven; preheat oven to 375°F. Have ready 2 or 3 ungreased cookie sheets.

4. Remove one disk of dough from refrigerator. Roll out dough between two sheets of wax paper to ¼-inch thickness. Remove top sheet. Cut dough with your favorite cookie cutters. Lift up excess dough and save for re-rolling. Using a metal spatula, transfer cutouts to ungreased cookie sheet, spacing about 1 inch apart. If cutouts vary in size, bake only identical or similar-size cutouts on the same sheet. Repeat procedure until all dough is used.

5. Bake one sheet at a time for 8 to 10 minutes, or until cookies are pale golden. Using a metal spatula, slide cookies onto wire racks and cool completely. Decorate cookies with any of the icings or glazes on pages 110–112 or devour unadorned. Store cookies in an airtight container.

Yield: 3 to 4 dozen cookies, depending on size of cookie cutter.

Raspberry Jam Sandwiches

1 recipe Traditional Butter
Cookies, (page 72), chilled
½ cup seedless raspberry jam

2 ounces semisweet chocolate,
melted

1.   Position rack in center of oven; preheat oven to 375°F. Have ready 2 or 3 ungreased cookie sheets.

2.   Remove one disk of dough from refrigerator. Roll out dough between two sheets of wax paper to ⅛-inch thickness. Cut dough into 2- or 2½-inch rounds or ovals. Lift up excess dough and save for re-rolling. Using a metal spatula, transfer cutouts to ungreased cookie sheets, spacing about 1 inch apart. Repeat procedure until all dough is used.

3.   Bake one sheet at a time for 6 to 8 minutes, or until cookies are pale golden. Using a metal spatula, slide cookies onto wire racks and cool completely.

4.   Spread jam over undersides of half the cookies. Top with remaining cookies, underside down. Dip a small spoon into melted chocolate and with it drizzle thin lines over cookies. Allow chocolate to harden before storing cookies. Store cookies between sheets of wax paper in an airtight container.

Yield: Approximately 25 cookies.

Sand Tarts

This recipe yields a large quantity of cookies, but you can freeze what you don't need for up to three months.

½ cup unsalted butter, softened
¾ cup granulated sugar
2 teaspoons grated lemon peel
2 large egg yolks
1 tablespoon milk
1 teaspoon vanilla extract
1¾ cups all-purpose flour

1 teaspoon baking powder
¼ teaspoon salt
1 beaten egg white
¼ cup granulated sugar
½ teaspoon ground cinnamon
Sliced almonds

COOKIE CUE

For a special treat, try toasting the almonds. To toast nuts in the oven, spread them in a single layer on a cookie sheet. Bake in a 325°F oven, stirring occasionally, for 10 to 15 minutes or until they are fragrant and look slightly browned. Remove at once. They burn quickly once browned.

1.   In a large bowl, and using an electric mixer set at medium speed, cream butter and sugar until light and smooth. Beat in lemon peel, about 30 seconds. Beat in egg yolks, milk, and vanilla until blended.

2.   In a medium bowl, stir together flour, baking powder, and salt. Add in thirds to creamed mixture, blending with a rubber spatula after each addition.

3.   Divide dough in half. Transfer each half to a sheet of plastic wrap, flatten into a thick disk, and wrap snugly. Chill 1 hour, or until firm enough to roll out. If dough is too firm, unwrap and allow to soften at room temperature for 5 to 10 minutes.

4.   Position rack in center of oven; preheat oven to 375°F. Lightly grease 2 or 3 cookie sheets.

5.   Remove one disk of dough from refrigerator. Dust work surface and rolling pin with flour, and roll out dough to ½-inch thickness. Cut dough with a 2- to 3-inch round cookie cutter. Lift up excess dough and save for re-rolling. Using a metal spatula, transfer cutouts to ungreased cookie sheets, spacing about 1 inch apart. Brush tops of cookies with egg white. Combine sugar and cinnamon in a small bowl; sprinkle about ½ teaspoon of mixture onto each cookie. Arrange 3 almond slices in center of each cookie. Repeat procedure until all dough is used.

6.   Bake one sheet at a time for 8 to 10 minutes, or until cookies are pale golden and brown around the edges. Remove cookie sheet to wire rack and cool 5 minutes. Using a metal spatula, slide cookies onto wire racks and cool completely. Store cookies in an airtight container.

Yield: Approximately 5 dozen cookies.

Black and White Flying Saucers

These large, soft cookies have been sold at deli counters and bakeries for more than forty years.

2¼ cups all-purpose flour
2 teaspoons baking powder
¼ teaspoon salt
½ cup unsalted butter, softened
¾ cup granulated sugar

1 large egg, at room temperature
1½ teaspoons vanilla extract
¼ cup milk
Chocolate Icing (page 110)
Vanilla Icing (page 110)

1. In a medium bowl, stir together flour, baking powder, and salt.
2. In a large bowl, and using an electric mixer set on medium speed, cream butter and sugar until light and smooth. Beat in egg and vanilla until fluffy. On low speed, gradually add flour mixture alternately with milk, blending well after each addition.
3. Divide dough in half. Transfer each half to a sheet of plastic wrap, flatten into a thick disk, and wrap snugly. Chill 1 to 2 hours, or until firm enough to roll out. If dough is too firm, unwrap and allow to soften at room temperature for 5 to 10 minutes.
4. Position rack in center of oven; preheat oven to 350°F. Have ready 2 or 3 ungreased cookie sheets.
5. Remove one disk of dough from refrigerator. Dust rolling pin and work surface with flour, and roll out dough to ¼-inch thickness. Cut dough with a 3½- to 4-inch round cookie cutter. Lift up excess dough and save for re-rolling. Using a metal spatula, transfer cutouts to cookie sheets, spacing about 1 inch apart. Repeat procedure until all dough is used.
6. Bake one sheet at a time for 8 to 10 minutes or until cookies are lightly browned on the bottom. Using a metal spatula, slide cookies onto wire racks and cool completely.
7. Spread Chocolate Icing over half of each cookie. Spread Vanilla Icing over other half of cookie. Let icings harden before storing cookies. Store cookies in an airtight container.

Yield: Approximately 20 cookies.

Pillow Cookies

These mildly spicy cookies are filled with apricot and coconut.

Cookie Dough

½ cup unsalted butter, softened
½ cup granulated sugar
2 teaspoons finely grated lemon
   peel
1 large egg, at room temperature
1 teaspoon vanilla extract

1½ cups all-purpose flour
½ teaspoon baking soda
½ teaspoon ground cinnamon
½ teaspoon ground ginger
¼ teaspoon ground cloves

Filling

½ cup finely chopped dried
   apricots
½ cup sweetened shredded or
   flaked coconut

3 tablespoons apricot preserves
Lemon Icing (page 110)

1.   *To prepare Cookie Dough:* In a large bowl, and using an electric mixer set on medium speed, cream butter and sugar until light and smooth. Beat in lemon peel, about 30 seconds. Beat in egg and vanilla until fluffy.

2.   In a small bowl, stir together flour, baking soda, cinnamon, ginger, and cloves. Add in thirds to creamed mixture, blending with a rubber spatula after each addition. Transfer dough to a sheet of plastic wrap, flatten into a thick disk, and wrap snugly. Chill 1 hour, or until firm enough to roll out. If dough is too firm, unwrap and allow to soften at room temperature for 5 to 10 minutes.

3.   Position rack in center of oven; preheat oven to 350°F. Have ready 2 or 3 ungreased cookie sheets.

4.   *To prepare Filling:* In a small bowl, stir together chopped apricots, coconut, and preserves.

5.   Dust work surface and rolling pin with flour. Roll out dough to ⅛-inch thickness. Cut dough with a 2½-inch round cookie cutter. Lift up excess dough and save for re-rolling. Using a metal spatula, transfer half the cutouts to cookie sheets, spacing about 1 inch apart. Spoon 2 rounded teaspoonfuls filling onto center of each cutout and top with another cutout. Press tines of a kitchen fork around edges to seal.

6.   Bake one sheet at a time for 8 to 10 minutes, or until cookie edges are firm and bottoms lightly browned. Using a metal spatula, slide cookies onto wire racks and cool completely.

7.   Dip a teaspoon into Lemon Icing and with it drizzle thin lines over cookies. Allow icing to harden before storing cookies. Store cookies in an airtight container.

Yield: Approximately 20 cookies.

Lemon-Honey Bears

These bear-shaped cookies are hard to resist.

½ cup unsalted butter, softened
⅓ cup granulated sugar
2 teaspoons finely grated lemon
   peel
3 tablespoons mild honey
1 large egg yolk

1⅓ cups all-purpose flour
½ teaspoon baking powder
⅛ teaspoon salt
Lemon Icing (page 110)
Raisins and/or small candies

COOKIE CUE

*Using a floured
cookie cutter, cut
rolled-out cookies
close together to get
as many cookies as
possible from the
first rolling. Too
much re-rolling
makes cookies
tough.*

1. In a large bowl, and using an electric mixer set on medium speed, cream butter and sugar until light and smooth. Beat in lemon peel, about 30 seconds. Beat in honey and egg yolk until blended.

2. In a medium bowl, stir together flour, baking powder, and salt. Add in thirds to creamed mixture, blending with a rubber spatula after each addition.

3. Divide dough in half. Transfer each half to a sheet of plastic wrap, flatten into a thick disk, and wrap snugly. Chill 1 hour, or until firm enough to roll out. If dough is too firm, unwrap and allow to soften at room temperature for 5 to 10 minutes.

4. Position rack in center of oven; preheat oven to 375°F. Have ready 2 to 3 ungreased cookie sheets.

5. Remove one disk of dough from refrigerator. Dust work surface and rolling pin with flour, and roll out dough to ⅛-inch thickness. Cut dough with a 2- to 3-inch teddy bear cookie cutter. Lift up excess dough and save for re-rolling. Using a metal spatula, transfer bears to ungreased cookie sheets, spacing about 1 inch apart. Repeat procedure until all dough is used.

6. Bake one sheet at a time for 8 to 10 minutes, or until cookies are pale golden and brown around the edges. Remove cookie sheet to wire rack and cool 2 minutes. Using a metal spatula, slide cookies onto wire racks and cool completely.

7. Pipe or spread Lemon Icing on bears and decorate with raisins and candies. Let icing harden before storing cookies. Store cookies in an airtight container.

Yield: 2 to 3 dozen cookies, depending on size of cutter.

Cookies Kids Like to Make

Giant Cookies

Kids love these king-size "pizza cookies."

½ cups unsalted butter, softened
1 cup firmly packed brown sugar
½ cup granulated sugar
1 large egg, at room temperature
¼ cup milk
1 teaspoon vanilla extract
1 cup all-purpose flour

½ teaspoon baking soda
½ teaspoon salt
¼ teaspoon cinnamon, optional
2½ cups quick old-fashioned oats
¾ cup chopped walnuts
M&M's plain chocolate candies

1.   Position rack in center of oven; preheat oven to 350°F. Line two 12- to 13¼-inch pizza pans with aluminum foil; lightly grease foil.

2.   In a large bowl, and using an electric mixer set at medium speed, cream butter and sugars until light and smooth. Beat in egg, milk, and vanilla until fluffy.

3.   In a small bowl, stir together flour, baking soda, salt, and cinnamon. Add in thirds to creamed mixture, blending with a rubber spatula after each addition. Stir in oats, walnuts, and ½ cup candies.

4.   Place about 2 cups dough onto each of the 2 prepared pizza pans. Spread dough to within 1 inch of edge of pan. Sprinkle each cookie with additional ⅓ cup candies. Bake one pan at a time for 15 to 17 minutes or until golden brown. Remove pan to wire rack and cool 10 minutes. Gently slide cookie with foil liner onto wire rack and cool completely. Cut into wedges or squares to serve. Store cookies in an airtight container.

Yield: Two 12- to 13¼-inch round giant cookies.

Note: If you don't have pizza pans, substitute two 17- by 14-inch foil-lined and greased cookie sheets for pizza pans. Spread dough to 11-inch diameter circle on each foil-lined cookie sheet. Bake as directed.

Variation: To make 4½-inch round jumbo cookies, omit pizza pans. Drop dough by level ⅓ cup measures onto greased cookie sheet, spacing about 4 inches apart. Bake at 350°F for 15 to 16 minutes or until lightly browned. Remove cookie sheet to wire rack and immediately press 4 to 6 candies firmly into warm cookies. Cool on cookie sheet 3 minutes. Using a metal spatula, slide cookies onto wire racks and cool completely. Store cookies in an airtight container.

Yield: Approximately 1 dozen cookies.

Kids' Cookie Dough

This dough is ideal for children when they want to mix, roll, and cut cookies quickly. It's not too sweet, and always makes delicious cookies.

½ cup unsalted butter, softened
⅓ cup confectioners' sugar
⅛ teaspoon salt
¾ teaspoon vanilla extract

1 cup all-purpose flour
Designer Cookie Paint (optional;
* page 112)*

1. Position rack in center of oven; preheat oven to 350°F. Have ready 2 large ungreased cookie sheets.

2. In a large bowl, and using an electric mixer set on medium speed, cream butter, sugar, and salt until light and smooth. Beat in vanilla until blended. Add flour in thirds, mixing with a rubber spatula after each addition.

3. Dust work surface and rolling pin with flour. Roll out dough to ½-inch thickness. Cut dough with your favorite cookie cutters. Lift up excess dough and save for rerolling. Using a metal spatula, transfer cutouts to ungreased cookie sheets, spacing about 1 inch apart. If cutouts vary in size, bake only identical or similar-size cutouts on the same sheet. Paint cookies with Designer Cookie Paint, if desired.

4. Bake one sheet at a time for 18 to 20 minutes, or until cookie bottoms are pale golden. Using a metal spatula, slide cookies onto wire racks and cool completely. Store cookies in an airtight container.

Yield: 2 to 4 dozen cookies, depending on size of cookie cutter.

C O O K I E C U E

Laundry detergent tops make perfect round cookie cutters. Tops from large containers are easy to handle, won't bend out of shape, and don't cost extra!

Thimble Cookies

Also known as Thumbprints, Jewels, and Gems, these cookies are fun to make, especially for children who like to poke their fingers into everything!

½ cup unsalted butter, softened
¼ cup granulated sugar
1 large egg yolk
¼ teaspoon almond extract
Pinch salt

1 cup all-purpose flour
1 large egg white, lightly beaten
¾ cup finely chopped walnuts
Any flavor jam or preserves

1. In a large bowl, and using an electric mixer set on medium speed, cream butter and sugar until light and smooth. Beat in egg yolk, almond extract, and salt until blended. Add flour in thirds, blending on low speed after each addition.

2. Position rack in center of oven; preheat oven to 350°F. Have ready 2 or 3 ungreased cookie sheets.

3. Pinch off pieces of dough and roll, one at a time, into 1-inch balls. Dip each ball in beaten egg white to coat, then roll in finely chopped walnuts. Arrange balls on ungreased cookie sheets, spacing about 1 inch apart. Using a thimble or your thumb or forefinger, make a hollow in the center of each cookie.

4. Bake one sheet at a time for 10 to 12 minutes, or until cookies are pale golden. Remove cookies from oven and gently press hollows again. Using a metal spatula, slide cookies onto wire racks and cool completely. Neatly fill each hollow with about ¼ teaspoon jam. For variety, fill each cookie with a different color jam. Store cookies in an airtight container.

Yield: Approximately 30 cookies.

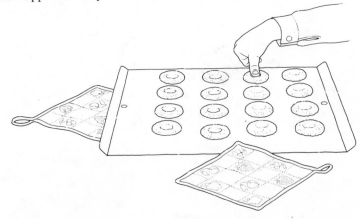

Snowballs

This no-bake cookie dough is perfect for little hands to mix together.

1 cup chunky peanut butter
¾ cup raisins
1 cup crisp rice cereal (such as
    Rice Krispies)
⅓ cup honey

⅓ cup unsweetened cocoa powder
1 teaspoon vanilla extract
2 cups unsweetened shredded or
    flaked coconut

1.   In a large bowl, and using a wooden spoon, stir together peanut butter, raisins, rice cereal, honey, cocoa, and vanilla until thoroughly blended. Pinch off pieces of dough and roll, one at a time, into 1½-inch balls.

2.   Spread coconut in bottom of a shallow pan. Roll balls, 6 or 7 at a time, in coconut to coat completely. Store cookies in an airtight container.

Yield: Approximately 36 cookies.

Crispy Jiffy Crunch Bars

Before arranging these on a cookie platter, place cut squares in colored muffin-tin papers for a festive look.

¼ cup unsalted butter or
   margarine
½ cup peanut butter
3 cups miniature marshmallows

½ teaspoon vanilla extract
4 cups crisp rice cereal (such as
   Rice Krispies)
1 cup raisins or peanuts

   1.   Line an 11- by 7-inch square baking pan with aluminum foil, allowing foil to extend 2 inches beyond two shorter sides of pan. Lightly grease bottom and sides of prepared pan.

   2.   Put butter and peanut butter in a large saucepan and stir constantly over low heat until smooth and combined. Add marshmallows, and continue stirring until melted. Remove pan from heat and stir in vanilla. Gradually add cereal, and mix until completely coated with marshmallow mixture. Stir in raisins or peanuts.

   3.   Press mixture evenly into prepared pan with a wooden spoon. Cool completely on a wire rack before cutting into squares.

Yield: 25 squares.

Forgotten Kisses

Put these cookies in the oven at night, and forget about them until the next morning.

2 egg whites, at room temperature
⅛ teaspoon cream of tartar
⅛ teaspoon salt
½ cup granulated sugar
1 teaspoon vanilla extract

¼ cup finely chopped almonds or walnuts
⅓ cup mini semisweet chocolate chips

1. Preheat oven to 350°F. Lightly grease a large cookie sheet.
2. In a large bowl, and using an electric mixer set on high speed, beat egg whites until just frothy. Add cream of tartar and salt, and beat until egg whites form soft peaks. Add sugar, 2 tablespoonfuls at a time, and beat until whites are stiff and glossy. Beat in vanilla. Sprinkle half the nuts and chocolate chips over surface and gently fold into mixture with a rubber spatula. Fold in remaining nuts and chips.
3. Drop slightly rounded teaspoonfuls of dough onto greased cookie sheet, spacing about 1 inch apart. Place cookie sheet in oven and *immediately turn off oven.* Allow cookies to ''bake'' in the warm oven 2 hours or overnight. Store cookies in an airtight container.

Yield: Approximately 36 cookies.

Honey Graham Crackers

1¾ cups whole wheat flour
1¼ cups all-purpose flour
1 teaspoon baking powder
½ teaspoon baking soda
¼ teaspoon ground cinnamon
Pinch salt

6 tablespoons unsalted butter,
  softened
⅔ cup firmly packed brown sugar
¼ cup honey
1 teaspoon vanilla extract
½ cup milk

1.   In a medium bowl, stir together whole wheat flour, all-purpose flour, baking powder, baking soda, cinnamon, and salt.

2.   In a large bowl, and using an electric mixer set on medium speed, cream butter and sugar until light and smooth. Beat in honey and vanilla until fluffy. On low speed, gradually add flour mixture alternately with milk, blending well after each addition.

3.   Divide dough in half. Flatten each half into a thick disk, and wrap each disk snugly in plastic wrap. Chill 1½ hours, or until firm enough to roll out. If dough is too firm to roll, unwrap and allow to soften at room temperature for 5 to 10 minutes.

4.   Position rack in center of oven; preheat oven to 350°F. Lightly grease 3 or 4 cookie sheets.

5.   Remove one disk of dough from refrigerator. Dust work surface and rolling pin with flour, and roll out dough to ⅛-inch thickness. Using a ruler and a knife, cut dough into 2¼-inch squares, or cut dough with a 2- to 3-inch cookie cutter. Using a metal spatula, transfer cutouts to greased cookie sheets, spacing about 1 inch apart. Prick each cutout 4 or 5 times with a fork. Repeat procedure until all dough is used.

6.   Bake one sheet at a time for 9 to 12 minutes, or until crackers are pale golden and edges are firm. Using a metal spatula, slide crackers onto wire racks and cool completely. Store crackers in an airtight container.

Yield: Approximately 42 crackers.

Wholesome Lunchbox Cookies

Peanut Butter–Honey Blossoms

A wholesome after-school snack your children won't turn down.

½ cup unsalted butter, softened
½ cup firmly packed brown sugar
½ cup creamy peanut butter
1 large egg, at room temperature
⅓ cup honey

2 teaspoons vanilla extract
2 cups all-purpose flour
¼ teaspoon baking soda
¼ teaspoon baking powder
1 cup coarsely chopped peanuts

1.   Position rack in center of oven; preheat oven to 350°F. Lightly grease 2 or 3 cookie sheets.

2.   In a large bowl, and using an electric mixer set on medium speed, cream butter and sugar until light and smooth. Beat in peanut butter, egg, honey, and vanilla until fluffy.

3.   In a small bowl, stir together flour, baking soda, and baking powder. Add in thirds to creamed mixture, blending with a rubber spatula after each addition.

4.   Pinch off pieces of dough and roll, one at a time, into 1½-inch balls. Arrange balls on greased cookie sheets, about 2 inches apart. Flatten each ball with a floured fork to make crisscross pattern. The cookies should be about ¼ inch thick. Press ¼ teaspoon chopped nuts into center of each cookie.

5.   Bake one sheet at a time for 10 to 12 minutes, or until cookies are lightly browned. Remove cookie sheet to wire rack and cool for 5 minutes. Using a metal spatula, slide cookies onto wire racks and cool completely. Store cookies in an airtight container.

Yield: Approximately 45 cookies.

Sunflower-Seed Cookies

This is a large, crisp cookie.

⅓ cup sunflower seeds,
   (approximately)
½ cup oil, preferably canola
⅔ cup firmly packed brown sugar
2 tablespoons molasses
1 large egg, at room temperature
1½ teaspoons vanilla extract

¾ cup all-purpose flour
¾ cup whole wheat flour
1 teaspoon baking soda
¼ teaspoon salt
1 cup uncooked quick-cooking
   rolled oats

1. Position rack in center of oven; preheat oven to 350°F. Lightly grease 1 or 2 cookie sheets. Place sunflower seeds in a small shallow bowl; set aside.

2. In a large bowl, and using an electric mixer set on medium speed, beat together oil, sugar, molasses, egg, and vanilla until thick and smooth.

3. In a small bowl, stir together flours, baking soda, and salt. Add in thirds to beaten mixture, blending with a rubber spatula after each addition. Stir in oats.

4. Pinch off pieces of dough and roll, one at a time, into 1½-inch balls. Press one side of each cookie into sunflower seeds. Arrange cookies (seeds should be on top) on greased cookie sheets, spacing about 2 inches apart. Bake one sheet at a time for 9 to 11 minutes or until cookies puff up and crack slightly. *Do not overbake.* Using a metal spatula, slide cookies onto wire racks and cool completely. Store cookies in an airtight container.

Yield: Approximately 2 dozen cookies.

Crispy Cinnamon Critters

½ cup unsalted butter, softened
½ cup packed brown sugar
1 large egg, at room temperature
1 teaspoon vanilla extract

1½ cups whole wheat flour
¾ cup graham cracker crumbs
1 teaspoon baking powder
½ teaspoon ground cinnamon

1. In a large bowl, and using an electric mixer set on medium speed, cream butter and sugar until light and smooth. Beat in egg and vanilla until fluffy.

2. In a small bowl, stir together flour, graham cracker crumbs, baking powder, and cinnamon. Add in thirds to creamed mixture, blending on low speed after each addition.

3. Divide dough in half. Flatten each half into a thick disk and wrap each disk snugly in plastic wrap. Chill 2 hours, or until firm enough to roll out. If dough is too firm to roll, unwrap and allow to soften at room temperature for 5 to 10 minutes.

4. Position rack in center of oven; preheat oven to 350°F. Have ready 2 or 3 ungreased cookie sheets.

5. Remove one disk of dough from refrigerator. Dust work surface and rolling pin with flour, and roll out dough to ⅛-inch thickness. Cut dough with a 2- to 3-inch animal cookie cutter. Lift up excess dough and save for re-rolling. Using a metal spatula, transfer cutouts to ungreased cookie sheets, spacing about 1 inch apart. Repeat procedure until all dough is used.

6. Bake one sheet at a time for 8 to 10 minutes, or until cookie edges are firm and bottoms are lightly browned. Using a metal spatula, slide cookies onto wire racks and cool completely. Store cookies in an airtight container.

Yield: Approximately 45 cookies.

Apricot-Glazed Fruit Chews

The shiny apricot glaze adds a special touch to this cereal cookie.

¼ cup unsalted butter
¼ cup unsweetened cocoa powder
⅓ cup honey
2¼ cups raisin bran cereal
½ cup toasted wheat germ

½ cup golden or dark raisins
½ cup chopped dried apricots
¼ cup apricot jam
⅓ cup sliced almonds

1. Melt butter in a heavy 2-quart saucepan over low heat. Remove pan from heat and whisk in cocoa until completely smooth. Stir in honey. Stir in cereal, wheat germ, raisins, and apricots with a wooden spoon.

2. Spoon 1 rounded teaspoon of mixture into miniature paper baking cups and arrange in a baking pan.

3. Stir apricot jam in a small, heavy pan over low heat until loose and liquidy, about 1 minute. Brush a thin layer of jam over cookie tops. Press 2 or 3 almond slices decoratively on top and chill cookies until set, about 1 hour.

Yield: Approximately 35 cookies.

Fig Bars

Good news! Fig bars are lower in fat than most other cookies.

Cookie Dough

½ cup unsalted butter, softened
⅓ cup granulated sugar
⅓ cup firmly packed brown sugar
2 large eggs, at room temperature
1 teaspoon vanilla extract

1⅓ cups all-purpose flour
1 cup whole wheat flour
¼ teaspoon baking soda
¼ teaspoon salt

Fig Filling

2 cups lightly packed dried figs
   (about 1 pound)
½ cup walnuts
½ cup firmly packed brown sugar

½ cup water
2 tablespoons orange juice
1 teaspoon grated orange peel

   1.   *To prepare Cookie Dough:* In a large bowl, and using an electric mixer set on medium speed, cream butter and sugars until light and smooth. Beat in eggs and vanilla until fluffy.
   2.   In a medium bowl, stir together flours, baking soda, and salt. Add in thirds to creamed mixture, blending with a rubber spatula after each addition.
   3.   Divide dough in half. Transfer each half to a sheet of plastic wrap, flatten each into a thick disk, and wrap each disk snugly. Chill 1 to 2 hours, or until firm enough to roll out. If dough is too firm, unwrap and allow to soften at room temperature for 5 to 10 minutes.
   4.   *To prepare Fig Filling:* In the bowl of a food processor fitted with a steel blade, grind together figs and walnuts. Scrape mixture into a 2-quart saucepan and add brown sugar, water, orange juice, and peel. Cook over medium heat, stirring constantly, until mixture boils and becomes very thick, 5 to 8 minutes. Remove pan from heat and cool mixture completely. When cool, divide into six equal portions.
   5.   Position rack in center of oven; preheat oven to 375°F. Lightly grease 2 cookie sheets.
   6.   Remove one disk of dough from refrigerator. Dust work surface and rolling pin with flour. Roll out dough to a 9- by 15- by ⅛-inch rectangle. Cut rectangle lengthwise into three equal strips. Spread one portion of filling down center of one strip. Using a long, narrow spatula, lift both sides of strip over filling, overlapping

edges slightly. With your fingers, press edges together lightly. Cut strip in half crosswise. Invert strips, one at a time, onto greased cookie sheet, spacing about 2 inches apart. Repeat procedure with remaining strips of dough. Chill strips in refrigerator, about 20 minutes, while you work with remaining dough.

7.   Bake one sheet at a time for 15 to 20 minutes, or until strips are lightly browned. Transfer cookie sheet to wire rack and cool 10 minutes. Using a metal spatula, slide strips onto wire racks and cool completely. Cut strips crosswise into 4 equal bars. Store bars in an airtight container.

Yield: 48 bars.

Chewy Fruity Granola Bars

Pack these into school lunchboxes, but save some for yourself!

2⅓ cups granola
1 cup coarsely chopped walnuts
¾ cup raisins
½ cup chopped dates
¼ cup chopped dried apricots
¾ cup sweetened shredded or
    flaked coconut

⅓ cup toasted honey wheat germ
½ cup unsalted butter
½ cup firmly packed brown sugar
⅓ cup honey
1 teaspoon vanilla extract

1. Position rack in center of oven; preheat oven to 350°F. Line a 9- by 12-inch baking pan with aluminum foil, allowing foil to overlap 2 inches beyond shorter sides of pan. Lightly grease bottom and sides of prepared pan.

2. In a large bowl, stir together granola, walnuts, raisins, dates, apricots, coconut, and wheat germ.

3. Put butter, sugar, and honey in a small, heavy pan and stir over low heat until butter melts and sugar dissolves. Remove pan from heat and stir in vanilla. Pour over granola mixture and stir with a wooden spoon until ingredients are thoroughly combined. Press mixture evenly into bottom of pan.

4. Bake for 20 minutes or until set. Remove pan to wire rack and cool completely. Use ends of foil to lift granola layer out of pan before cutting into bars. Store bars in an airtight container.

Yield: Approximately 36 bars.

Lemon-Iced Zucchini Bars

Cookie Dough

¾ cup unsalted butter, softened
¾ cup granulated sugar
¼ cup firmly packed brown sugar
1 tablespoon finely grated lemon
　peel
2 large eggs, at room temperature
1 teaspoon vanilla extract
1¾ cups all-purpose flour

1½ teaspoons baking powder
¼ teaspoon salt
2 cups coarsely shredded, unpeeled
　zucchini
¾ cup unsweetened shredded or
　flaked coconut
½ cup chopped pitted dates
1 cup chopped raisins

Lemon Icing

2 tablespoons unsalted butter,
　softened
2 tablespoons fresh lemon juice

¼ teaspoon ground cinnamon
1 cup confectioners' sugar
1 cup finely chopped walnuts

1.　*To prepare Cookie Dough:* Position rack in center of oven; preheat oven to 350°F. Line a 10- by 15-inch jelly-roll pan with aluminum foil, allowing foil to overlap 2 inches beyond shorter sides of pan. Lightly grease bottom and sides of prepared pan.

2.　In a large bowl, and using an electric mixer set on medium speed, cream butter and sugars until light and smooth. Beat in lemon peel, about 30 seconds. Beat in eggs and vanilla until fluffy.

3.　In a small bowl, stir together flour, baking powder, and salt. Add in thirds to creamed mixture, blending at low speed after each addition. Stir in zucchini, coconut, dates, and raisins. Spread batter evenly in prepared pan and smooth top with a rubber spatula.

4.　Bake for 30 to 35 minutes, or until a toothpick inserted in center comes out clean. Transfer pan to wire rack and cool 15 minutes.

5.　Meanwhile, prepare Lemon Icing: In a small bowl, beat together butter, lemon juice, cinnamon, and sugar until smooth. Spread icing over warm layer and sprinkle walnuts over top. Cool completely. Use ends of foil to lift zucchini layer out of pan before cutting into bars. Store bars in an airtight container.

Yield: 48 bars.

Orange-Glazed Carob Brownies

These brownies are delicious straight out of the freezer.

⅓ cup canola or safflower oil
½ cup carob powder
3 large egg whites, at room
  temperature
¾ cup firmly packed brown sugar
1 teaspoon vanilla extract
½ cup unbleached flour

¾ teaspoon baking powder
½ teaspoon cinnamon
1 teaspoon finely grated orange
  peel
½ cup chopped walnuts
½ cup raisins
Orange Glaze (see page 111)

1.   Position rack in center of oven; preheat oven to 350°F. Line a 9-inch square baking pan with aluminum foil, allowing foil to overlap 2 inches beyond two opposite sides of pan. Lightly grease bottom and sides of prepared pan.

2.   In a large bowl, and using an electric mixer set on medium speed, beat oil, carob powder, egg whites, sugar, and vanilla until thick and smooth, about 2 minutes.

3.   In a medium bowl, stir together flour, baking powder, cinnamon, and orange peel. Add in thirds to carob mixture, blending at low speed after each addition. Stir in walnuts and raisins. Spread batter in prepared pan and smooth surface with a rubber spatula.

4.   Bake for 17 to 20 minutes, or until a toothpick inserted in center comes out with a few moist crumbs. Remove pan to wire rack and cool 10 minutes. Spread Orange Glaze over warm brownies. Cool completely. Use ends of foil to lift brownie layer out of pan before cutting into bars or squares. Store brownies in an airtight container at room temperature in the refrigerator or freezer.

Yield: 16 bars.

Holiday Cookies

Favorite Holiday Sugar Cookies

Use this old-fashioned sugar-cookie recipe when you want to cut out holiday trees, balls, bells, or other festive shapes.

1 cup unsalted butter, softened
1¼ cups confectioners' sugar
1 large egg, at room temperature
1½ teaspoons vanilla extract

2¼ cups all-purpose flour
1 teaspoon baking soda
1 teaspoon cream of tartar
¼ cup granulated sugar

COOKIE CUE

For an attractive decoration, use a clean, small paintbrush to spread light corn syrup on top of or around edges of baked cookies. Dip cookies or just edges in colored sugar or sprinkles.

1.　In a large bowl, and using an electric mixer set on medium speed, cream butter and confectioners' sugar until light and smooth. Beat in egg and vanilla until fluffy.

2.　In a medium bowl, stir together flour, baking soda, and cream of tartar. Add in thirds to creamed mixture, blending at low speed after each addition.

3.　Divide dough in half. Flatten each half into a thick disk, and wrap each disk snugly in plastic wrap. Chill 1½ hours, or until firm enough to roll out. If dough is too firm to roll, unwrap and allow to soften at room temperature for 5 to 10 minutes.

4.　Position rack in center of oven; preheat oven to 350°F. Lightly grease 3 or 4 cookie sheets.

5.　Remove one disk of dough from refrigerator. Dust work surface and rolling pin with flour, and roll out dough to ¼-inch thickness. Cut dough with your favorite cookie cutters. Lift up excess dough and save for re-rolling. Sprinkle granulated sugar evenly over cutouts. Using a metal spatula, transfer cutouts to ungreased cookie sheets, spacing about 1 inch apart. Repeat procedure until all dough is used.

6.　Bake one sheet at a time for 6 to 8 minutes, or until cookie edges just start to turn a light brown. Using a metal spatula, slide cookies onto wire racks and cool completely. Store cookies in an airtight container.

Yield: 4 to 5 dozen cookies, depending on size of cookie cutter.

Spritz Cookies

Homemade Spritz cookies look as professional as bakery cookies, but they taste much better!

1 cup unsalted butter, softened
2/3 cup granulated sugar
1 large egg, at room temperature
1 teaspoon vanilla extract
1/2 teaspoon almond extract
2 1/4 cups all-purpose flour

1/2 cup finely ground blanched
   almonds
1/4 teaspoon salt
Colored sugar, dragées, or glacé
   cherries, optional

1.   In a large bowl, and using an electric mixer set on medium speed, cream butter and sugar until light and smooth. Beat in egg, vanilla, and almond extract until fluffy.

2.   In a medium bowl, stir together flour, nuts, and salt. Add in thirds to creamed mixture, blending with a rubber spatula after each addition. The dough should be soft, but not sticky. If necessary, add up to 1/4 cup more flour.

3.   Position rack in center of oven; preheat oven to 350°F. Have ready 3 or 4 ungreased cookie sheets. Attach desired template to a cookie press and fill cookie press with dough.

4.   Press out dough onto ungreased cookie sheets, spacing pressed dough about 1 1/2 inches apart. If first cookie does not hold its shape, chill dough until firm enough to press easily. Decorate cookies if desired.

5.   Bake one sheet at a time for 10 to 12 minutes, or until cookies are pale golden. Do not let cookies brown. Using a metal spatula, slide cookies onto wire racks and cool completely. Store cookies in an airtight container.

Yield: Approximately 60 cookies.

Mini Fruitcake Cookies

These cookies stay moist if stored airtight, so you can make them well in advance of the holiday season.

¼ cup unsalted butter, softened
½ cup firmly packed brown sugar
2 large eggs, at room temperature
¼ cup honey
1 teaspoon vanilla extract
1½ cups all-purpose flour
2 teaspoons baking soda

½ teaspoon ground cinnamon
½ teaspoon ground cloves
½ teaspoon ground nutmeg
1 cup coarsely chopped walnuts
1 cup currants
1 cup chopped glacé cherries or
*   mixed glacé fruit*

1. Position rack in center of oven; preheat oven to 300°F. Lightly grease 3 or 4 cookie sheets.

2. In a large bowl, and using an electric mixer set on medium speed, cream butter and sugar until light and smooth. Beat in eggs, honey, and vanilla until fluffy.

3. In a small bowl, stir together flour, baking soda, cinnamon, cloves, and nutmeg. On low speed, gradually add half the flour mixture to creamed mixture, blending well after each addition. Stir walnuts, currants, and cherries or mixed fruit into remaining flour mixture; gradually stir into dough until thoroughly blended.

4. Drop rounded teaspoonfuls of dough onto greased cookie sheets, spacing about 2 inches apart. Bake one sheet at a time for 15 to 20 minutes, or until centers spring back when lightly touched. Using a metal spatula, slide cookies onto wire racks and cool completely. Store cookies in an airtight container.

Yield: Approximately 60 cookies.

Pfeffernusse

Store "pepper nuts" airtight with an apple slice, if you want them to stay fresh for several months.

2 large eggs, at room temperature
1 cup granulated sugar
1 teaspoon finely grated lemon
   peel
1/4 cup finely chopped almonds
2 cups all-purpose flour
1/2 teaspoon baking powder

1/2 teaspoon ground cinnamon
1/2 teaspoon ground cloves
1/2 teaspoon ground ginger
1/2 teaspoon ground cardamom
1/4 teaspoon freshly ground pepper
Vanilla Confectioners' Sugar (page
   112)

1. Position rack in center of oven; preheat oven to 325°F. Lightly grease 2 or 3 cookie sheets.

2. In a large bowl, and using an electric mixer set on medium speed, beat eggs until light in color. With mixer on high speed, gradually add sugar, beating until mixture is very thick and light, about 5 minutes. Beat in lemon peel, about 30 seconds. Beat in almonds.

3. In a small bowl, stir together flour, baking powder, cinnamon, cloves, ginger, cardamom, and pepper. Add in thirds to egg mixture, blending with a rubber spatula after each addition.

4. Pinch off pieces of dough and roll, one at a time, into 1-inch balls. Arrange balls on greased cookie sheets, spacing about 2 inches apart.

5. Bake one sheet at a time for 13 to 18 minutes, or until cookies are lightly browned on the bottom. Using a metal spatula, slide cookies onto wire racks and cool completely.

6. Put Vanilla Confectioners' Sugar in a sturdy plastic bag, add 4 or 5 cookies at a time, and shake until cookies are completely coated. Store cookies in an airtight container with an apple slice for at least 1 week to soften and ripen.

Yield: Approximately 46 cookies.

Hamantaschen

Hamantaschen are traditionally eaten on the Jewish holiday Purim.

Poppy Seed Filling

½ cup poppy seeds
¼ cup orange juice or water
3 tablespoons honey
¼ cup raisins

¼ cup finely chopped walnuts,
  optional
½ teaspoon grated lemon peel

Cookie Dough

⅓ cup vegetable oil
¾ cup granulated sugar
3 large eggs, at room temperature
2 teaspoons grated orange peel

1 teaspoon vanilla extract
3¼ cups all-purpose flour
1 tablespoon baking powder
½ teaspoon salt

1. *To prepare Poppy Seed Filling:* Grind poppy seeds in a spice mill or blender until fine. In a small saucepan over low heat, stir together ground poppy seeds, orange juice or water, honey, and raisins. Cook for 10 to 15 minutes, stirring frequently to prevent mixture from sticking to pan. When mixture thickens and pulls away from sides of pan, remove pan from heat and set aside to cool. When cool, stir in chopped nuts and lemon peel. Cover with plastic wrap until needed.

2. *To prepare Cookie Dough:* In a large bowl, and using an electric mixer set on medium speed, beat oil, sugar, eggs, orange peel, and vanilla until thick, about 3 minutes.

3. In a medium bowl, stir together flour, baking powder, and salt. Add in thirds to egg mixture, blending at low speed after each addition.

4. Position rack in center of oven; preheat oven to 350°F. Lightly grease 2 or 3 cookie sheets.

5. Shape dough into a smooth ball. Divide dough into quarters and cover with a kitchen towel. Dust work surface and rolling pin with flour and roll out one quarter of the dough to ⅛-inch thickness. Cut dough with a 3- to 3-½-inch round cookie cutter. Lift up excess dough and save for re-rolling.

6. Spoon 1 rounded teaspoon of filling into center of each cutout. Working with one cutout at a time, lift edges up and in toward the center and pinch together in three places to form a triangle. The filling should be visible in the center. Arrange triangles on greased cookie sheets, spacing about 2 inches apart. Repeat with remaining dough.

7.   Bake one sheet at a time for 12 to 15 minutes, or until cookies are lightly browned around the edges. Using a metal spatula, transfer cookies to wire racks and cool completely. Store cookies in an airtight container.

Yield: Approximately 36 cookies.

Note: Poppy seed filling may be used immediately, or stored in the refrigerator in a tightly covered jar for up to 3 months.

Claire's Ruggies (Rugulach)

Ruggies are Claire Feingold's affectionate term for rugulach. Because the dough is so rich, Claire advises chilling it overnight.

Dough

1 cup unsalted butter, softened
1 8-ounce package cream cheese, softened
⅓ cup granulated sugar
1 teaspoon vanilla extract
½ teaspoon salt
2 cups all-purpose flour

Raspberry-Nut Filling and Topping

½ cup granulated sugar
½ teaspoon ground cinnamon
¾ cup raspberry jam
⅓ cup granulated sugar
½ chopped walnuts
2 cups raisins
¼ cup milk

1.   *To prepare Dough:* In a large bowl, and using an electric mixer set on medium speed, beat together butter and cream cheese until blended and perfectly smooth. Beat in sugar and vanilla until thoroughly blended. Beat in salt. With mixer on low speed, add flour in thirds, mixing just until blended after each addition.

2.   Divide dough into quarters. Flatten each quarter into a thick disk and wrap each disk snugly in plastic wrap. Chill at least 4 hours, or overnight. If dough is too firm to roll, unwrap and allow to soften at room temperature for 5 to 10 minutes.

3.   Position rack in center of oven; preheat oven to 350°F. Lightly grease 2 or 3 cookie sheets of a size that will fit in your refrigerator.

4.   Combine the ½ cup sugar and ½ teaspoon cinnamon in a small dish until evenly blended.

5.   Remove one disk of dough from refrigerator. Dust work surface and rolling pin with flour. Roll dough into a circle approximately 9 inches in diameter. Using a small spatula, spread 2 tablespoons raspberry jam evenly over dough. Cut circle into 14 equal pie-shaped wedges.

6.   In a small bowl, stir together the ⅓ cup sugar, walnuts, and raisins. Sprinkle a quarter of nut filling over cut surface and press down gently with the back of a teaspoon. Starting at wide edge, roll each wedge tightly. Brush milk over each rugulach and dip into cinnamon-sugar topping. Arrange rugulach point side down on greased cookie sheets, spacing about 1½ inches apart. Repeat procedure with remaining dough.

When cookie sheet is filled with rugulach, cover with plastic wrap and chill for 30 minutes or until rugulach are firm.

7. Bake one sheet at a time for 15 to 20 minutes, or until rugulach are lightly browned. Using a metal spatula, slide rugulach onto wire racks and cool completely. Store rugulach in an airtight container.

Yield: 56 rugulach.

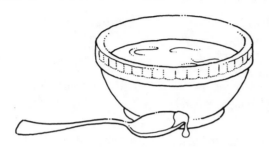

Gingerbread Kid Cookies

Lois Knerr teaches at The Columbia Greenhouse Preschool in New York City. Every year, Lois and her four-and five-year-old students make these mildly spicy cookies. They are the best gingerbread cookies I've ever tasted.

½ cup granulated sugar
1½ cups molasses
1 cup unsalted butter, softened
1 large egg, at room temperature
1 teaspoon ground ginger
1 teaspoon ground cinnamon

¾ teaspoon salt
2 teaspoons baking soda dissolved
  in ¼ cup boiling water
4 cups all-purpose flour
Vanilla Icing (optional; page 110)

1.   In a large bowl, and using an electric mixer set on medium speed, beat sugar, molasses, and butter until smooth and well blended. On low speed, beat in egg, ginger, cinnamon, salt, and dissolved baking soda until blended. Add flour, one cup at a time, mixing until just blended after each addition.

2.   Divide dough into quarters. Flatten each quarter into a thick disk and wrap each disk snugly in plastic wrap. Chill 2 hours, or until firm enough to roll out. If dough is too firm to roll, unwrap and allow to soften at room temperature for 5 to 10 minutes.

3.   Position rack in center of oven; preheat oven to 350° F. Have ready 3 or 4 ungreased cookie sheets.

4.   Dust work surface and rolling pin with flour. Remove one disk of dough from refrigerator and roll to ¼-inch thickness. Cut with a 4- to 6-inch gingerbread-person cookie cutter. Lift up excess dough and save for re-rolling. Using a metal spatula, transfer cutouts to ungreased cookie sheet, spacing about 1 inch apart. Repeat procedure until all dough is used.

5.   Bake one sheet at a time for 8 to 10 minutes, or until cookies feel firm. Using a metal spatula, slide cookies onto wire racks and cool completely. Decorate with Vanilla Icing or devour unadorned. Store cookies in an airtight container.

Yield: 2 to 3 dozen, depending on size of cookie cutter.

Aunt Gussie's Walnut Snowballs

My friend Wendie Wallis remembers her aunt Gussie baking these rich, delicate cookies during the holidays. These cookies make great gifts.

¾ cup unsalted butter, softened
⅓ cup confectioners' sugar
1 teaspoon vanilla extract
¼ teaspoon almond extract
½ cup finely chopped walnuts

2 cups all-purpose flour
¼ teaspoon baking powder
Pinch salt
Confectioners' sugar

1.   Position rack in center of oven; preheat oven to 325°F. Lightly grease 2 cookie sheets.

2.   In a large bowl, and using an electric mixer set on medium speed, cream butter and sugar until light and smooth. Stir in vanilla and almond extracts and chopped walnuts.

3.   In another bowl, stir together flour, baking powder, and salt. Add in thirds to creamed mixture, mixing with a rubber spatula after each addition. Pinch off pieces of dough and roll, one at a time, into 1-inch balls. Arrange balls on ungreased cookie sheets, spacing about 1 inch apart.

4.   Bake one sheet at a time for 15 to 17 minutes, or until cookies are pale golden. Do not let cookies brown. Remove cookie sheet to wire rack and cool for 2 or 3 minutes. Using a metal spatula, transfer 6 or 7 cookies to a shallow baking pan and generously sift confectioners' sugar over cookies to coat completely. Transfer cookies to wire racks and cool completely. Repeat until all cookies have been coated. Sift additional confectioners' sugar over cookies before serving. Store cookies in an airtight container.

Yield: Approximately 40 cookies.

Almond Buttercrunch Toffee Squares

1 cup unsalted butter, softened
1 cup firmly packed brown sugar
1 large egg yolk
1 teaspoon vanilla extract
1 cup all-purpose flour

¾ teaspoon ground cinnamon
¼ teaspoon salt
2 cups semisweet chocolate chips
1 cup finely chopped blanched
  almonds

1.   Position rack in center of oven; preheat oven to 325°F. Line a 10- by 15-inch jelly-roll pan with aluminum foil, allowing foil to overlap 2 inches beyond shorter sides of pan. Lightly grease bottom and sides of prepared pan.

2.   In a large bowl, and using an electric mixer set on medium speed, cream butter and sugar until light and smooth. Beat in egg yolk and vanilla until blended.

3.   In a small bowl, stir together flour, cinnamon, and salt. Add in thirds to creamed mixture, blending with a rubber spatula after each addition. Spread batter into prepared pan and smooth surface.

4.   Bake for 20 to 25 minutes, or until golden brown. Remove pan to wire rack and immediately sprinkle chocolate chips over hot surface. Wait 10 minutes for chips to soften before spreading them evenly over surface. Sprinkle almonds on top and gently press into chocolate with your fingertips. Chill 15 minutes, or just until chocolate hardens. Use ends of foil to lift toffee layer out of pan before cutting into 1½-inch squares. Store squares in an airtight container.

Yield: Approximately 60 squares.

Icings, Glazes, and Other
Cookie Decoration Ideas

Chocolate Icing

1 ounce semisweet chocolate
2 tablespoons butter
2 tablespoons granulated sugar
1 tablespoon light corn syrup

Pinch salt
2 tablespoons heavy cream
1 teaspoon cornstarch
½ teaspoon vanilla extract

1. Combine chocolate, butter, sugar, corn syrup, and salt in a small, heavy saucepan. Cook over low heat, stirring occasionally, until chocolate and butter melt and sugar dissolves. Remove from heat.
2. Stir together heavy cream and cornstarch until well blended, then pour into chocolate mixture. Cook over medium heat, stirring constantly, until mixture begins to boil. Remove from heat and stir in vanilla. Cool icing in pan 5 minutes, stirring occasionally, before spreading over cooled cookies.

Yield: About ½ cup.

Vanilla Icing

1¼ cups confectioners' sugar
2 tablespoons milk
1 teaspoon vanilla extract

In a small bowl, combine confectioners' sugar, milk, and vanilla, stirring until smooth. The icing should be fluid, but thick enough to form a line when drizzled from the tip of a teaspoon. If necessary, add a few drops of milk to thicken, or a little more confectioners' sugar to thin the icing.

Yield: Approximately ½ cup.

For Lemon Icing: Omit milk and substitute 2 tablespoons fresh lemon juice and 1 teaspoon finely grated lemon peel.

Yield: Approximately ½ cup.

Buttercream Icing

This icing is ideal for spreading or piping. Tint with food coloring for added appeal.

¼ cup unsalted butter, softened　　*1 tablespoon milk*
1 cup confectioners' sugar
1 teaspoon vanilla extract or fresh
　lemon juice

In a small bowl, and using an electric mixer set on low speed, beat together all ingredients until fluffy. Spread or pipe on cookies. Allow icing to harden on cookies before storing.

For Chocolate Buttercream Icing: Melt 2 squares unsweetened chocolate. Cool chocolate slightly before beating into icing.

Yield: Approximately 1 cup.

Orange Glaze

1 tablespoon unsalted butter,　　*1¼ cups confectioners' sugar*
　softened　　　　　　　　　　*2 tablespoons orange juice*
1 teaspoon grated orange peel

In a small bowl, combine butter, orange peel, and confectioners' sugar. Stir in orange juice until icing is smooth and spreadable.

Yield: Approximately ½ cup.

Vanilla Confectioners' Sugar

You can use vanilla-flavored sugar whenever a recipe calls for plain sugar. It can also be used to flavor whipped cream or to sweeten berries or other fruits.

2 vanilla beans
1 box confectioners' sugar

Split vanilla beans in half lengthwise with a small, sharp knife. Put beans in a jar or container and spoon in confectioners' sugar. Cover airtight and allow sugar to absorb vanilla flavor for at least 48 hours. Replenish sugar as needed for up to one year before discarding beans. The sugar lasts in the airtight container indefinitely.

For Vanilla Granulated Sugar: Substitute granulated sugar for confectioners' sugar, using about 4 cups of sugar.

Designer Cookie Paint

2 egg yolks   *Assorted food coloring*
1 teaspoon water

Lightly beat together egg yolks and water in a small bowl. Divide mixture into 3 or 4 other small bowls and add a few drops food coloring to create desired color. Use a clean small paintbrush to paint cookies.

Yield: Approximately ¼ cup.

Index